Schriftenreihe zur Justizforschung Band 2

Yves Emery
Lorenzo G. De Santis
Vera Hertig

Peut-on manager la justice ?
Kann man die Justiz managen?
Can we manage the Judiciary?

Schriftenreihe zur Justizforschung

Schriftenreihe zur Justizforschung Band 2

Peut-on manager la justice ?

Kann man die Justiz managen?

Can we manage the Judiciary?

Prof. Dr. Yves Emery
MSc Lorenzo G. De Santis
MA Vera Hertig

Stämpfli Verlag
Nomos
Jan Sramek Verlag

Die Studie wurde im Rahmen des Forschungsprojekts «Grundlagen guten Justizmanagements in der Schweiz» (www.justizforschung.ch) erstellt.

Mit freundlicher Unterstützung des Schweizerischen Nationalfonds zur Förderung der wissenschaftlichen Forschung.

FNSNF
SCHWEIZERISCHER NATIONALFONDS
ZUR FÖRDERUNG DER WISSENSCHAFTLICHEN FORSCHUNG

Die Aufsätze in diesem Buch unterlagen einem Peer-Review.
Les articles ont été soumis à un Peer-Review.
The articles were peer-reviewed.

Bibliografische Information der Deutschen Nationalbibliothek
Die Deutsche Nationalbibliothek verzeichnet diese Publikation in der Deutschen Nationalbibliografie; detaillierte bibliografische Daten sind im Internet über http://dnb.d-nb.de abrufbar.

ISBN 978-3-8487-2971-5

ISBN 978-3-7097-0091-4

Dieses Werk ist in unserem Buchshop unter www.staempfliverlag.com erhältlich.

ISBN Print 978-3-7272-7672-9
ISBN Judocu 978-3-0354-1288-8
ISBN E-Book 978-3-7272-5935-7

FSC
www.fsc.org
MIX
Papier aus verantwortungsvollen Quellen
FSC® C016087

Inhaltsverzeichnis

Introduction

Depuis les années 1980 au niveau international, le management a fait son entrée dans les administrations publiques, univers traditionnellement imprégné d'une logique avant tout juridique. Une entrée que certains redoutaient parce qu'elle posait l'hypothèse d'une mort possible de l'organisation publique, réputée éternelle dans l'inconscient collectif.[1] On imagine aisément que l'incursion du management au sein de la justice, institution essentielle de tout Etat démocratique et d'une certaine façon «au-dessus» de la mêlée, se présentant «hors du temps et hors du monde»[2], pose des questions encore plus fondamentales, sur l'opportunité et la pertinence même d'une telle idée, mais également sur le risque d'une forme de *banalisation* de l'institution judiciaire, qui pourrait être assimilée à une organisation productive comme une autre, dénaturant la noblesse du travail judiciaire.[3] 1

D'un autre côté, les tribunaux doivent faire face à une masse de travail grandissante, à une complexification des affaires et à des exigences toujours plus pressantes de la part des différentes *parties prenantes* de la justice, à commencer par les justiciables eux-mêmes, qui comparent aujourd'hui les services fournis par la justice à d'autres prestations de l'administration, voire du secteur privé: flexibilité, rapidité, sens du service et des relations humaines sont quelques-unes des qualités attendues des services publics.[4] Sans compter la réactivité et la transparence attendue par les médias et plus généralement les citoyens, questionnant à la faveur d'affaires récentes dramatiques[5] le fonctionnement-même de la justice et la redevabilité des juges en particulier. 2

Prise en étaux entre l'indépendance constitutionnelle qui en est au fondement, et la redevabilité (accountability) face à la population -et plus spécifiquement puisqu'il s'agit d'une particularité helvétique, face aux commissions parlementaires chargées d'en exercer la haute surveillance- la justice s'ouvre quelque peu malgré elle à des considérations relevant du 3

1 SANTO/VERRIER (1993).
2 VIGOUR (2008).
3 VIGOUR (2008).
4 EMERY (2009), FRANCE QUALITÉ PUBLIQUE (2006).
5 Voir l'affaire «Marie» qui a défrayé la chronique en Suisse romande http://www.24heures.ch/vaud-regions/faits-divers/contenu-2/meurtre-de-marie/s.html, consulté le 18.06.2015.

registre managérial.[6] Une ouverture qui pose de nombreuses questions techniques, telles que la fixation d'objectifs aux juges ou encore l'analyse de leur charge de travail[7], mais plus fondamentalement questionne la *réceptivité culturelle* de la justice, et des juges en particulier, au management. C'est le thème que nous avons décidé d'approfondir et qui fait l'objet de cet ouvrage.

4 Pourquoi mettre le projecteur sur la dimension culturelle du projet de *managérialisation* de la justice? Plusieurs raisons peuvent être avancées, à commencer par la connaissance développée depuis de nombreuses décennies sur les processus de changement organisationnel, qui montre combien la variable culturelle est décisive dans le succès des projets de changement.[8] C'est ensuite la prise de conscience progressive que la nouvelle gestion publique (NGP), véritable déferlante sur les administrations suisses dès le milieu des années 1990, représente un projet culturel par excellence, en ce que la NGP véhicule de nouveaux paradigmes et de nouvelles valeurs, contrastant de manière radicale avec celles du modèle bureaucratique.[9] Dans le cadre d'une institution telle que la justice, où le droit est au cœur-même de l'activité et représente le socle constitutionnel, pour ne pas dire ontologique, de sa raison d'être, on mesure la difficulté d'introduire une approche managériale qui véhicule des valeurs nouvelles telles que l'efficience et l'efficacité, plutôt que le respect des règles et de la procédure : le choc culturel est programmé ! C'est enfin parce que les tribunaux représentent l'archétype de ce que Mintzberg appelle la *bureaucratie professionnelle*[10], une forme d'organisation où les professionnels – en l'occurrence les juges et plus généralement les juristes, notamment les greffiers - occupent une place prépondérante à tous les niveaux de la hiérarchie. En effet, la caractéristique principale de ces organisations est liée au pouvoir que la catégorie formée par les professionnels exerce en leur sein: du fait de leur expertise unique au centre des processus de production – ici la jurisprudence- les professionnels maîtrisent non seulement le cœur stratégique[11] de l'organisation, mais également les postes-clés régissant la conduite de celle-ci. A l'image d'autres bureaucraties profession-

---

6 KETTIGER (2003).
7 LIENHARD/KETTIGER (2009).
8 SAINSAULIEU (1983), SCHEIN (1992).
9 MEYER/HAMMERSCHMID (2006), MÖNKS (1998), SCHEDLER/PROELLER, (2007).
10 MINTZBERG (1989).
11 Kerngeschäft, core business.

nelles dirigées par des spécialistes telles que les hôpitaux ou les universités, les tribunaux sont ainsi dirigés par des juges, contribuant par hypothèse à la prégnance de la logique juridique dans le traitement de toutes les affaires de direction, y compris celles liées à des considérations de bonne organisation ou de gestion des ressources.

L'expression «par hypothèse» prend tout son sens ici, puisque c'est précisément la question de recherche qui sous-tend les trois contributions de cet ouvrage: «quelle est la réceptivité culturelle de la justice, et plus spécifiquement des organisations du pouvoir judiciaire, aux pratiques et outils de management public?» La culture, les valeurs et attentes liées à une bonne justice relèvent-elles aujourd'hui avant tout du registre juridique, ou incorporent-elles des caractéristiques du registre managérial? Et les juges eux-mêmes, exerçant ce rôle noble et essentiel dans toute démocratie mettant en avant l'indépendance du troisième pouvoir, voient-ils un potentiel dans les outils de management et sont-ils ouverts à leur mise en œuvre au sein de leur tribunal? Et plus généralement, peut-on penser qu'à l'avenir il sera possible de «manager les juges», comme on manage les employés d'une entreprise commerciale, tant il est vrai qu'il est difficilement concevable d'introduire une logique managériale au sein de la justice sans encadrer les magistrats? 5

Une littérature croissante illustre la résistance des professionnels à tout effort de managérialisation[12], en particulier pour les professionnels engagés au sein d'organisations (par opposition aux indépendants) qui tentent de défendre leur autonomie dans un carcan gestionnaire toujours plus contraignant[13]. On peut d'autant plus anticiper cette résistance pour les juges, puisque ces derniers bénéficient de la garantie constitutionnelle de leur indépendance en qualité de magistrat «disant le droit», laquelle ne saurait être remise en cause, quelle que soit la rationalité managériale avancée. 6

Pour répondre à ces questions, les trois analyses de cet ouvrage présentent en détail les méthodes utilisées et passent en revue la littérature actuelle, avant de discuter les résultats obtenus au sein des tribunaux de l'ensemble des cantons romands, ainsi que de deux cantons Suisses alémanique et du Tessin. A ce stade introductif, précisons que les démarches 7

12 Ferlie/Geraghty (2007), Kirkpatrick/Ackroyd/Walker (2005), Sehested (2002).
13 Evetts (2009).

analytiques mobilisées combinent à la fois une approche quantitative basée sur des questionnaires diffusés à large échelle, permettant des analyses statistiques approfondies, et une approche qualitative fondée sur un programme de plus de 80 entretiens auprès des acteurs-clés de la justice, permettant une analyse fine des propos tenus par les personnes interviewées.

8 La première étude compare les attentes des juges et des managers de tribunaux[14] en ce qui concerne leur vision d'une bonne justice, et en quoi ces attentes répondent, en partie au moins, à la perception de la justice par la population suisse. Après avoir montré la progression de la nouvelle gestion publique au sein du pouvoir judiciaire et mis l'accent sur la dimension culturelle des tribunaux, à l'exemple d'études internationales sur cette question, les auteurs discutent de l'incontournable interaction entre le processus judiciaire et le processus managérial, ainsi que des relations entre juges et managers de tribunaux, en relevant les différences culturelles portées par ces acteurs et les relations de pouvoir qui peuvent en découler. Ils plaident ensuite pour une approche *macro-culturelle* de la culture du troisième pouvoir, incluant les valeurs et attentes tant d'acteurs internes qu'externes aux tribunaux, en particulier des citoyens-justiciables. Basés sur 18 entretiens semi-directifs de juges et de managers de tribunaux, ainsi que sur une enquête représentative menée auprès de la population suisse, l'analyse développée compare les principales attentes formulées par les juges et les managers, leurs convergences et divergences, et montre que les logiques les plus fréquemment mobilisées relèvent autant du registre civique que du registre commercial (au sens de Boltanski & Thévenot, voir ci-après), dénotant ainsi une certaine hybridité de la culture actuelle du pouvoir judiciaire. Parmi les nombreux résultats, la perception de la population fait ressortir un décalage important avec les acteurs de la justice sur deux attentes essentielles (d'une bonne justice), à savoir la célérité et le caractère compréhensible.[15] Cette analyse permet de cibler les actions managériales prioritaires susceptibles d'être introduites ainsi que la réceptivité des acteurs internes à de telles initiatives.

9 La seconde étude porte sur les freins culturels au management de la justice en Suisse. Elle analyse le discours que les acteurs – tout particulièrement les juges- tiennent sur les pratiques de management, les valeurs,

[14] Court managers.
[15] «understandable».

représentations, habitudes et manières de penser qui ressortent des quelque 80 entretiens réalisés à cet effet. Après avoir fait un tour de la littérature sur les différentes conceptions de la culture, organisationnelle et institutionnelle, et présenté les principaux arguments sous-tendant le choc potentiel entre culture juridique et managériale, les auteurs développent les nombreux arguments révélés par les entretiens et susceptibles d'expliquer les freins à la *managérialisation* de la justice. Des arguments liés autant à la spécificité de la justice en général, des tribunaux et du travail des juges et de leur personnalité en particulier, qu'à l'inadéquation supposée des concepts et outils de management au travail de la justice. Il est relevé notamment que les managers, là où ils ont été introduits «ne connaissent ou ne comprennent pas l'activité des juges», et que de toute manière, les juges son intouchables autant qu'incontrôlables. On mesure alors le chemin qu'il reste à parcourir pour convaincre les juges du bien-fondé des outils de management, et surtout la nécessité d'adapter ceux-ci aux caractéristiques constitutives de l'activité judiciaire.

La dernière étude pose encore plus directement la question du mana- 10
gement des juges, en détaillant les opportunités et défis liés à la conduite des magistrats exerçant ce rôle-clé au cœur du pouvoir judiciaire. Partant de l'affirmation maintes fois relayée par la littérature spécialisée, selon laquelle un leadership efficace et entrepreneurial est une condition essentielle à une justice efficace et efficiente, l'étude se focalise sur la conduite directe des magistrats et ne traite donc pas de la conduite politique (haute surveillance du pouvoir judiciaire). Elle passe tout d'abord en revue l'abondante littérature sur le leadership en général, et plus spécifiquement sur le leadership au sein des organisations publiques, des bureaucraties professionnelles (telles que la justice) ainsi que du pouvoir judiciaire. En synthèse, l'étude résume les questions-clés suivantes: «qui» peut conduire les juges? «Sur quelles responsabilités» peut porter cet encadrement? «Comment» s'y prendre? Et «pourquoi» développer cette pratique? Sur cette base, les auteurs analysent les propos tenus par les juges ainsi que d'autres acteurs centraux de la justice (internes et externes, tels que responsables politiques, avocats et journalistes) lors de 56 interviews semi-directifs. Il en ressort que la conduite des juges ne sera un succès que si elle respecte la culture professionnelle des juges. Pour ce faire, les auteurs formulent et discutent quelques thèses provocatrices concernant la conduite des juges, par exemple le fait que les juges ne peuvent pas être dirigés puisqu'ils n'ont pas de supérieur hiérarchique. Il en ressort qu'une pratique de conduite informelle et collégiale est certes souhaitable, mais

pas suffisante: une structure ainsi qu'une conduite minimales permettraient de clarifier la situation actuelle et de décharger les juges, notamment dans les domaines organisationnel et administratif, mais cela nécessiterait de la part des personnes exerçant ce rôle de réelles qualités de leadership, mobilisant un style participatif, plus transformationnel et instrumental que transactionnel.

11 Au final, le but poursuivi par cette étude en trois volets, au-delà des questions de recherche formulées ci-dessus, est de mieux comprendre les caractéristiques culturelles des tribunaux afin d'apprécier la meilleure façon d'introduire des pratiques de management au sein de cette institution, tout en respectant les valeurs à la base de son fonctionnement. En effet, toute initiative de management imposée par les instances dirigeantes de la justice est vouée à l'échec si elle n'intègre pas cette dimension essentielle de son identité organisationnelle et institutionnelle. Comme le montrent Ferlie et al, les pratiques de management seraient alors susceptibles d'être «digérées» par les professionnels-juges, qui en neutraliseraient tout effet concret dans leurs pratiques quotidiennes.[16] Or nous avons la conviction que pour faire face aux défis toujours plus nombreux et complexes auxquels la justice doit faire face, l'introduction d'une logique managériale appropriée et adaptée au contexte culturel de la justice est non seulement nécessaire, mais indispensable, contrairement à certains qui y voient un cheval de Troie susceptible d'annihiler, à terme, l'indépendance de la justice et des juges. Mais comme l'explique Pichault en mobilisant une approche *contextualiste* du changement organisationnel, celui-ci a d'autant plus de chances de succès qu'il s'inscrit en cohérence par rapport à la culture en place et que les démarches concrètes qui le concrétisent sont elles-mêmes articulées de manière cohérente entre elles, en soutien aux défis que l'organisation entend relever.[17]

12 Gageons que les constats et analyses développés par les trois contributions de cet ouvrage contribuent, dans un registre moins juridique ou technique que les analyses traditionnellement réalisées à cet égard, à mieux saisir les enjeux et facteurs de succès d'une introduction *intelligente* des pratiques managériales au sein des tribunaux.

---

[16] FERLIE/GERAGHTY (2007).
[17] PICHAULT (2009).

Literature de l'introduction

Emery, Y. (2009). L'apport du management de la qualité au renouveau du modèle bureaucratique. Revue de l'Innovation, 14(3), 1-24.

Evetts, J. (2009). New Professionalism and New Public Management: Changes, Continuities and Consequences. Comparative Sociology, 8(2), 247-266.

Ferlie, E., & Geraghty, K. J. (2007). Professionals in Public Services Organizations. Implications for Public Sector "reforming". In E. Ferlie, L. E. Lynn & C. Pollitt (Eds.), The Oxford Handbook of Public Management (pp. 422-445). Oxford: Oxford University Press.

France Qualité Publique. (2006). Evaluer la qualité et la performance publiques. Paris: La documentation française.

Kettiger, D. (2003). Wirkungsorientierte Verwaltungsführung in der Justiz (Vol. 44). Bern: Société suisse des sciences administratives.

Kirkpatrick, I., Ackroyd, S., & Walker, R. (2005). The New Managerialism and Public Service Professions. Basingstoke: Palgrave McMillan.

Lienhard, A., & Kettiger, D. (2009). Geschäftslastbewirtschaftung bei Gerichten: Methodik, Erfahrungen und Ergebnisse einer Studie bei den kantonalen Verwaltungs und Sozialversicherungsgerichten. ZBL.

Meyer, R., & Hammerschmid, G. (2006). Public Management Reform: An Identity Project. Public Policy and Administration, 21(1), 99-115.

Mintzberg, H. (1989). Le management, voyage au centre des organisations. Paris: Les Editions d'Organisation.

Mönks, J. (1998). La nouvelle gestion publique: boîte à outils ou changement paradigmatique? In M. Hufty (Ed.), La pensée comptable (pp. 77-89). Genève/Paris: Les Nouveaux Cahiers de l'IUED/PUF.

Pichault, F. (2009). Gestion du changement. Perspectives théoriques et pratiques. Bruxelles: de Boeck.

Sainsaulieu, R. (1983). La régulation culturelle des ensembles organisés. L'Année sociologique, 33, 195-217.

Santo, V.-M., & Verrier, P. E. (1993). Le management public. Paris: PUF.

Schedler, K., & Proeller, I. (Eds.). (2007). Cultural Aspects of Public Management Reform. Oxford, UK: Elsevier.

Schein, E. (1992). Organizational Culture and Leadership. San Francisco: Jossey Bass.

Sehested, K. (2002). How new public management reforms challenge the roles of professionnals. International Journal of Public Administration, 25(12), 1513-1537.

Vigour, C. (2008). Ethos et légitimité professionnels à l'épreuve d'une approche managériale: le cas de la justice belge. Sociologie du travail, 50, 71-90.

Court managers and judges about "good" justice: Their main expectations and how they fit with the perceptions of the Swiss population

Authors

Lorenzo Gennaro De Santis, PhD candidate, IDHEAP (Swiss Graduate School of Public Administration), University of Lausanne

Yves Emery, Professor, IDHEAP (Swiss Graduate School of Public Administration), University of Lausanne

Abstract

Today's increasing managerial control over the third power may lead to deep and profound changes in the judicial culture and to a complexification/hybridization of its values. Except from a reduced number of American studies,[1] very few has been published on the culture of the Judiciary. Hitherto, we could not find any studies focusing on the judicial culture of Switzerland but ours.[2] Nonetheless, we believe Switzerland is a very special and interesting case as, contrary to what is sometimes argued, Switzerland has its own administrative culture(s)[3] and probably a distinct judicial culture as well.[4]

This article aims at a better understanding of the institutional culture of the Judiciary in Switzerland by discovering what "good justice" means nowadays in this country. It seeks to define whether and to which extent the views of "good justice" of judicial actors (judges without managerial experience), managerial actors (court managers) and external actors (citizens) are similar, and to what extent the expectations of court managers and judges incorporate management-oriented values.

As judges are at the heart of the judicial system and exert a strong influence on other groups of actors,[5] the congruence of their expectations with those of court managers and the perceptions of citizens will be at the core of the analysis. Based on semi-structured interviews of judges and court managers on one hand, and on a representative survey by Swiss

1 BROWN (2006), CHURCH (1985), OSTROM/HANSON/KLEIMAN (2005).
2 EMERY/DE SANTIS (2014).
3 GIAUQUE (2013).
4 DE SANTIS (2015).
5 SULLIVAN/WARREN/WESTBROOK (1994).

citizens on the other, this article compares and discusses the qualities of "good justice" in Switzerland.

1. Introduction

1 Modernization strategies inspired by the New Public Management (NPM)[6] movement and quality management initiatives recently flowed into tribunals and courts. These strategies, which consider the Judiciary as a *Public Service*,[7] do not challenge a basic principle of the justice system, that judges are constitutionally independent and must be able to work freely from any source of influence.[8] However, judicial organizations must be properly administrated in order to improve their efficiency, their efficacy and their accountability,[9] without damaging the quality of judicial decisions and their "client" orientation. Thus, management should complement judicial work to reinforce the quality of justice as there would be no "good justice" without good court management, despite the fact that the judicial and the managerial processes are frequently seen as being fundamentally incompatible.

2 In practice, however, the proper interaction between judicial work and court management seems far more complex than expected.[10] In the 90's, Stupak encouraged "teamwork" between judges and managers as (judicial) substance shouldn't be separated from administration since managerial leadership would become the critical element to improve court performance, efficacy and productivity in the near future.[11] Even before the establishment of NPM some authors already pointed out, when talking

---

6 NPM comes from the merger of two opposites: the new institutional economics which focuses on public choice, transaction costs and principal agent theories on the one hand and on "business-type managerialism in the public sector, in the tradition of the international scientific management movement" on the other. Put differently, NPM is the result of the application of microeconomics theory to the bureaucratic environment coupled with managerial techniques used in the private sector (HOOD, 1991, P. 5-6).

7 "There is no good justice, as independent as it can be, as long as it is not oriented towards litigants" (BOILLAT/LEYENBERGER, 2008, P.58), freely translated from French by the authors.

8 BERNDT (2010), KLOPFER (2007), LANGBROEK (2008).

9 LIENHARD (2009).

10 AMRANI-MEKKA (2008), LIENHARD/BOLZ (2001), VAUCHEZ (2008).

11 STUPAK (1991).

about the relationship between judges and court managers, that the problem comes from an inevitable conflict between the goals, values and functions of each group.[12] This reinforces the need to analyse whether justice should accommodate perceptions and expectations from other stakeholders of the judicial system like politicians, the media, lawyers and especially citizens.

As judges are at the centre of the Judiciary[13] and have a strong influence on other groups of actors,[14] the congruence of their expectations with those of court managers, will be at the heart of the analysis. The fact that work relationships are sometimes strained between judges and court managers[15] will drive us to investigate whether their expectations are similar or not. Additionally, this article will also explore how these expectations fit with the perception of justice by the citizens, as an indicator of the congruence between internal and external actors' views of the Judiciary. 3

Therefore, the research questions addressed in this paper are the following: 4

a. What are the divergences and convergences when it comes to the expectations[16] of "good justice" according to judges without managerial responsibilities and court managers? 5

b. How close are these expectations to the perceptions of the Swiss population? 6

c. How do these expectations fit with management-oriented values? 7

We will first define the contextual background in which the research takes place prior to summarizing the literature on judicial organisations and management, before zooming more specifically on the culture of the Judiciary and explaining the reasons that incited us to undertake this study. Afterwards, we will describe our methodology and present the results and conclusions. 8

---

12 CAMERON/ZIMMERMANN/DOWLING (1987).

13 Institutional reproduction is often associated with the demands of dominant agents (i.e. judges) within organizational fields (POWELL/DIMAGGIO (1991).

14 SULLIVAN et al. (1994).

15 LANGBROEK (2008), DELVAUX (2010).

16 By expectations we mean "normative expectations" is the sense of what "ought" to happen in the Judiciary to have a "good justice" according to the actors interrogated instead of what "would" normally happen (SUGDEN, 1998), P.74. We are indebted to anonymous reviewer for this remark.

2. Contextual background: NPM and court management in Switzerland

9 First, it is probably useful to rapidly remind how the Swiss Judiciary is organised.[17] In 2012, the Swiss Judiciary represented 2.2 billion € of annual spending (or 1.4% of total public spending, below the European average of 2.2%). In total, this represents 359 tribunals, 1271 professional judges, 2873 lay judges, 839 prosecutors and 5569 administrative and other staff.[18] It is a quite complex institution as both the Confederation and the 26 cantons have their own judicial systems. At the Federal level, the Judiciary includes the Federal Supreme Court and the federal courts of first instance.[19] At the cantonal level, which is the focus of our research, each of the 26 cantons has its own constitution, parliament, government and court system. In both criminal and civil cases, there are generally two judicial levels in each canton: district courts serving as courts of first instance and cantonal ones serving as courts of appeal.[20] When it comes to public law disputes, specialised administrative courts decide on appeals against decision of the cantonal administration, as "in Switzerland disputes between citizens and the government are considered not as civil law proceedings but as a separate area of law".[21] The decisions of the cantonal and administrative courts can be appealed to the Federal Supreme Court in any case.

As for the NPM movement, it appeared in the 90's in Switzerland, as 10
a reaction to the perceived weaknesses of public sector organisations (input-oriented, rules predominance, etc.), and to the excessive political control of operative decisions.[22] The main objectives were to increase the performance of public services in terms of efficiency and effectiveness[23] and to foster their customer-orientation.

---

17 The following depiction is largely inspired by KIENER (2012).

18 Including clerks and other non-judges positions, CEPEJ (2014).

19 These consist of: The Federal Criminal Court, the Federal Administrative Court and a number of specialised courts. We will not go into the details as our study focuses on the cantonal courts. The interested reader can refer to KIENER (2012).

20 In addition, there are a number of specialised courts such as juvenile, tenancy, commercial or labour courts whose rules and regulations vary widely across cantons.

21 KIENER (2012), P. 407.

22 SCHEDLER (2003), LIENHARD/BOLTZ /RITZ/STEINER/LADNER (2005).

23 EMERY/MARTIN (2010).

The Swiss context is rather receptive to private sector methods and values[24] and the reforms conducted in the country include, among other things, the search of an increased efficiency, a decentralisation process, the flattening of hierarchies together with the introduction of performance contracts between politicians (principal) and public managers (agent).[25] 11

However, the implementation of NPM programmes happened at a much reduced pace than anticipated.[26] Many promoters of public sector reforms deeply underestimated the importance of administrative culture and the institutional[27] dimension of reforms in Switzerland,[28] considering NPM only as a set of managerial techniques. In that respect, it is not surprising that the Judiciary[29] has been one of the latest institutions to have experienced NPM.[30] Nevertheless, a cultural change seems to happen in Switzerland's court management practices. To give a few examples: in the canton of Vaud, second instance judges (Tribunal cantonal) failed to be elected by the political authority as they were believed to lack some of the necessary competences for the positions to be filled,[31] showing a shift from political affiliation and a traditional routinized election towards desired skills. Similarly, the recent issues of an overloaded justice system in Fribourg brought back court administration in the spotlight.[32] Finally, the management of the justice system in Geneva was heavily criticized by a recent report published by the Court of Auditors.[33] 12

Although still scarce, a nascent literature exists on court management in Switzerland. It focuses on reforms from the perspective of constitution- 13

---

24 THOM/RITZ (2013).

25 SCHEDLER (2003).

26 EMERY /GIAUQUE (2012).

27 We believe, as the new institutionalists do, that institutions are "first and foremost products of human action", and that their larger environment composed of cultural elements must be considered to understand them, since an institution is a macro level abstraction. That is why we will analyse the Judiciary as an institution in our quest to understand it, POWELL/DIMAGGIO (1991), P. 28.

28 GIAUQUE (2013).

29 For an overview of the Swiss judicial system, see KIENER, 2012.

30 WIPFLI (2006).

31 http://www.arcinfo.ch/fr/suisse/vaud-les-candidats-au-tribunal-cantonal-tous-recales-566-1197103 [last consulted on 28.06.2013].

32 http://www.rts.ch/info/regions/fribourg/4980074-la-justice-fribourgeoise-fonctionne-bien-mais-est-surchargee.html [19.06.2013].

33 http://www.cdc-ge.ch/fr/Publications/Rapports-d-audit/2012.html [11.07.2013], report Nr.54.

al and administrative law,[34] on organisational, structural and leadership aspects of the court,[35] on the effects of the recent unification of Swiss procedural laws, on the organisation of the tribunals,[36] or on the implementation of NPM instruments into courts following the reorganisation of judicial institutions.[37] Additionally, certain authors investigated the degree of autonomy required for court administration to guarantee the independence of the Judiciary[38] or the way courts' workload is managed.[39] Moral dilemmas and stress experienced by judges were also investigated by some scholars.[40] In the end, we could not find any publication dedicated to court culture, or more specifically to the comparison of expectations of judges and court managers regarding good justice with the perception of the population in Switzerland.

3. Theoretical background and review of the literature

3.1 The Judiciary and the (New) Public Management

14 Politicians often justify the use of NPM methods to achieve good management of state funds. Indeed, public organisations are accountable to the taxpayers and governments for the way they utilize their resources.[41] NPM approaches also intend to increase the legitimation of public institutions by improving their efficiency and rendering them more valuable for the population (see the "Value for money" initiatives, launched for example in the UK).[42] This may also be the case in the Judiciary, as the quality of a judicial norm, a trial or a judgement can't be differentiated from the quality of their elaboration processes and consequently from a good organisation of judicial entities.[43] As a consequence, opposing judicial and management processes of courts is pointless,[44] un-

34 LIENHARD (2011), POLTIER (2011).
35 MOSIMANN (2011), POLTIER (2011), WIPFLI (2006).
36 CANTON DE BERNE (2011).
37 CANTON DE BERNE (2011).
38 POLTIER (2012/3).
39 LIENHARD /KETTIGER (2009).
40 LUDEWIG (2009).
41 LANGBROEK (2005).
42 MOORE (1995).
43 CADIET (2011), PAULIAT (2007).
44 KIRAT (2010), PAULIAT (2005).

derpinning that judges and court managers should collaborate to improve the overall quality of courts.

Nonetheless, the generalization of NPM is not straightforward as "dif- 15
ferent administrative values have different implications for fundamental aspects of administrative design"[45] highlighting the importance to take into account the specificities of each entity. Overall, what Hamel calls the managerial model[46] can't be imported as a one size fits all solution but has to be tailored in order to fit with the goals and the culture of the concerned institution. This argument is especially relevant for the Judiciary, which has a strong professional and administrative culture mainly inspired by traditional public administration values such as legality, equality, objectivity, impartiality and general interest.

NPM encountered many problems when applied to the Judiciary in 16
general and to judges in particular. For example, evaluation standards and indicators are not just instruments, since they are supposed to echo what is considered essential and valuable for the internal actors of the courts. These values, expectations and quality criteria have to be internalized by judges and can't be imposed by management but by professional experts who are used to the organisation of the Judiciary and to the aspirations of stakeholders.[47] Even those favouring the introduction of managerial techniques in the Judiciary believe indicators must be chosen carefully and their pertinence unanimously recognized in order to be accepted by all.[48]

Furthermore, NPM must not be considered only as a technical project, 17
but as a cultural initiative too,[49] which may neglect some fundamental principles of justice such as freedom and equality.[50] The underestimated cultural dimension of NPM obviously explains at least partly the difficulties encountered by its implementation in the Judiciary.[51] In fact, values such as efficiency, efficacy, productivity, customer-orientation, or even return on investment, are far from being prevalent in the Judiciary, and

---

45 Hood (1991), p. 9.
46 Hamel (2011).
47 Böttcher (2004), Langbroek (2005).
48 Vicentini (2011).
49 Bezes (2007), Schedler/Proeller (2007).
50 Frydman (2011).
51 Lienhard (2009).

may lead to a cultural shock as it happened in other administrative contexts.[52]

18 The dependency of magistrates to court administrators[53] may also be amplified as managerial knowledge is often missing in the judicial context. In this respect, it seems crucial to adopt a commonly accepted definition of an efficient court, and in a larger sense, of good justice.[54]

3.2 What do we know about the culture of the Judiciary?

3.2.1 General concepts and determinants of "culture"

19 Swidler[55] (1986) quoted by Powell & DiMaggio (1991) says "culture represents a tool kit from which people select both institutionalized ends and the strategies for their pursuit". Put differently "cultural frames establish approved means and define desired outcomes"[56] of any institution reinforcing the idea that culture is paramount when it comes to understanding their functioning.

20 The determinants of culture are several and there is usually no uniform culture in one institution but a mosaic of (sub-) cultures.[57] During the seventies and eighties, scholars pointed out the importance of the national level,[58] as well as the organizational one through the notion of organisational or corporate culture.[59] More recently, Bouckaert classifies culture from a public administration point of view in four categories: Macro (civilisation, place and structure), Meso (professional administration), Micro (organisational level) and Nano (offices, job clusters).[60] Others put the emphasis on multiple levels and define administrative culture as an aggregate of various aspects such as social values, economic and political cultures and other sources of influence.[61] Generally speaking, institutions (as the Judiciary) strongly contribute to shape the culture of any organisation

---

52 GIAUQUE/ EMERY (2008), RONDEAUX (2011).
53 SCHMETZ (2006).
54 WIPFLI (2006).
55 SWIDLER (1986).
56 POWELL/DIMAGGIO (1991), P. 28.
57 MATZ/ADAMS/WILLIAMSON (2011).
58 HOFSTEDE (1980).
59 DEAL/KENNEDY (1982), SCHEIN (1990).
60 BOUCKAERT (2007).
61 DWIVEDI/GOW (1999).

(court), as they represent a continuous sociological interaction process between actors who enact the values, norms and objectives related to their mission.[62] That is the reason why, in this article, we will adopt an institutional approach of what we call the judicial culture by analysing the common expectations of various actors from several courts across Switzerland.

3.2.2 Focusing on Judicial culture

Knowledge about culture within the Judiciary is scarce. Comparative research has been done in several countries,[63] and also focused on specific (court) organisations.[64] Most of them try to explain the link between court culture and performance,[65] therefore considering culture as an antecedent and as an instrument to boost court productivity. 21

Previous studies investigating the culture of the Judiciary rarely included external stakeholders (media, citizens etc.), but only analysed the relationships between internal actors of courts (lawyers, judges, attorney, litigants etc.). Even though Eisenstein & Flemming[66] mention the idea of a national culture and common values, the core of their research is on county legal culture, which they describe as the values and perceptions of the principal members of the court community about how they are expected to act and how they believe they do act in reality when performing their tasks. Other scholars only consider informal relations between judges, lawyers, defense attorneys and prosecutors in their research.[67] More recently, some authors based their conceptualisation of court culture on the relevancy of cooperation and coordination between judges, prosecutors and defence attorneys in the efficient resolution of criminal affairs.[68] This is presumably linked to the assumption that getting the consent of internal stakeholders is more important than the one of others.[69] What Church calls the local legal culture[70] is this mix of attitudes and practices which influ- 22

---

62 BLOOR/DAWSON (1994), HALL/TAYLOR (1996), POWELL/DIMAGGIO (1991).
63 BELL (2006), VIGOUR (2006).
64 OSTROM/ OSTROM/HANSON/KLEIMAN (2005).
65 OSTROM/ OSTROM/HANSON/KLEIMAN (2007), MATZ et al. (2011).
66 EISENSTEIN/FLEMMING/NARDULLI (1988).
67 CHURCH/CARLSON/LEE/TAN (1978).
68 OSTROM/HANSON (1999).
69 LANGBROEK (2005).
70 CHURCH (1985).

ence, among others, the pace of litigation and corresponds to Bouckaert's meso and micro levels. In this regard, the cultural dimension of courts is vital, as it is one of the pivotal factors related to a successful implementation of managerial values and techniques into the judicial sphere. Burke and Broccolina[71] attempted to integrate both approaches, arguing that court culture as defined by Ostrom[72] is complementary to the local legal culture conceptualized by Church,[73] but none really insisted on comparing the views of court managers and judges. The adoption of a broader perspective, including the views of those two crucial actors, will allow us to analyse the institutional culture of the Judiciary.

3.2.3 Judges and court managers

23 Judges, notably more than any other public servants, have a very strong common identity as they are educated as members of a group of remarkable professionals.[74] Broadening the influence of new role expectations from different internal and external actors (e.g. politicians, citizens, lawyers, attorneys, clerical and managerial staff) that potentially conflict with judges' professional ethos and their vision of "good justice" may gradually transform the culture of the Judiciary, leading to probable value clashes. Professional standards of judges and managerial expectations of court administrators may indeed contradict each other.[75]

24 Despite the fact that justice management is often regarded as being subordinated to the Judiciary, management-related expectations to good justice may have a non-negligible influence on it,[76] including the length of trials[77] and the quality of judgements. As for court administrators, if we except the study of Cameron & Zimmermann produced prior to the NPM era,[78] they are rarely considered as actors who influence court culture, although they are probably those with the best helicopter-view of court organisation, practices and values.

---

71 BURKE/BROCCOLINA (2005).
72 OSTROM et al. (2005).
73 CHURCH (1985), CHURCH (1982).
74 LANGBROEK (2005).
75 EMERY /GIAUQUE (2012), FORTIER/EMERY (2012), KIRKPATRICK et al. (2005).
76 KIRAT (2010), POLTIER (2012/3).
77 PALUMBO/GIUPPONI/NUNZIATA/MORA SANGUINETTI (2013).
78 CAMERON et al. (1987).

Giving more managerial power to certain judges may lead to bad management and induce problems regarding the independence of some judges towards those who consider the new management as nothing else than a sophisticated way to retain power.[79] Legendre quoted in Jeuland, even goes further putting in direct opposition management and law. In all cases, the additional problem of the blurring frontiers between judicial and administrative duties has to be acknowledged.[80] 25

Some authors highlight another antagonism by opposing the efficiency of the tribunal and the institution itself, defending the idea that judicial life is now more focused on the former rather than on the way the organisations of the Judiciary and the social relations within them function.[81] Similarly, Mattijs say judges try to please the chiefs of courts in a way or the other, when their work is appraised on quantitative standards only[82] and some drifts can consequently be expected.[83] Justice should therefore be managed in such a manner that the economical rationality don't interfere with the Judiciary.[84] If those spheres mix up, there is a risk that the use of the scarcity of resources' concept would weaken the rational-legal foundation of the administrative bureaucracy, which guarantees judicial security.[85]

This may explain why judges tend to appoint court administrators who are "non-threatening individuals who will not actively seek reform or disturb the status quo".[86] But these practices are changing. The relationship between the President of a Belgian court and its new human resources advisor evolved from the withdrawal of the former HR advisor, due to the lack of legitimacy of his position, to "the shared conviction of the complementarity of the two functions, which together with trust and mutual support, will lead to a true partnership for a common and shared construction".[87] Nevertheless, the introduction of NPM-like techniques still leads to cultural resistance, by further polarizing the relations between judges 26

79 JEULAND (2011), LABRUSSE-RIOU (2011).
80 POLTIER (2012/3).
81 LABRUSSE-RIOU (2011).
82 MATTIJS (2006).
83 PIRAUX/BERNARD (2006).
84 ROUSSEAU (2011).
85 SERVERIN (2011).
86 BERKSON/HAYS (1977), P. 87.
87 Freely translated from French by the authors, DEWART/LEROY (2013), p. 22.

and court managers. The expectations of both actors are essential but not sufficient to fully apprehend the cultural context of the Judiciary, leading us to explore the perception of external stakeholders as well.

3.3 From a micro (organisational) to a macro (institutional) perspective of Judicial culture including various stakeholders.

27 The few studies which look at the judicial culture actually focus on its micro level. In our opinion, it is crucial to broaden the scope of the analysis by including the perceptions of external stakeholders (media, citizens etc.) if one wants to carefully grasp the culture of the Judiciary, although we are aware that studying the microlevel foundation of an institution is far from being trivial.[88] This argument is not only based on the mainstream literature related to "new public governance",[89] but also on the fact that organizations belonging to the Judiciary are gradually becoming open systems, which interact more and more with their environment. In that sense, we will concentrate in the remaining paragraphs on the institutional culture of the Judiciary, which we consider as a macro perspective of the judicial culture encompassing the common characteristics of the courts it is made of.

28 In order to understand the institutional culture of the Judiciary, perceptions and influences exerted by external stakeholders of courts must be further analysed. If we define the Judiciary as a public service, as mentioned in the introduction, the perceptions of the citizens are then of premier importance as they may shape the judicial institution in an era where the legitimacy of public administration is increasingly linked to user-satisfaction. Indeed, justice could gain a lot if jurists would listen to what non-jurists have to tell them.[90] Stupak for example believes it is critical that external stakeholders get acquainted with the culture of the courts.[91] In addition, Coolsen shows that stakeholders' attitudes are essentials in the delay reduction of disposition case in criminal justice courts, which evidently has an indirect effect on the quality of justice.[92] A research cen-

---

88 ZUCKER (1991).
89 OSBORNE (2006); BUDD (2007).
90 GARAPON (2000).
91 STUPAK (1991).
92 COOLSEN (2008).

tred on quality court management showed introducing external parties such as prosecutors, defense counsel and the users of courts (e.g., the parties and witnesses) leads to more improvements of court functioning than otherwise,[93] demonstrating that other external stakeholders should be considered as they impact the Judiciary.

Recently, an OECD report said external factors such as cultural ones influence the "demand" for justice and the trial length of civil cases.[94] Few decades ago, in a comparison of the most expeditious US criminal courts with slower ones, scholars developed the notion of Judicial Syndrome which is the result of a particular interpersonal behaviour.[95] According to this study, legal and social systems in the United States render people willing to please and impress judges. The consequence of this judicial syndrome is that judges don't have a clear-sighted view of themselves and the world around them and thus agents of change, who frequently are court administrators, are required.[96] 29

On the importance of including more specifically the citizens in the understanding of the institutional culture of the Judiciary, Nardulli defines the local legal culture articulated by Church, Carlson & al.[97] as a subset of political culture, which is itself a component of the environmental context in which the judicial subsystem exists.[98] He specifies that internal aspects of the courts are correlated to the three dimensions of political culture, that is to say the role of the government, public policies' orientations and the legal system. Among the factors of the local political culture influencing the internal functioning of state courts in the USA, the author quotes the influence of the electorate, social pressure and the socialisation of judges.[99] 30

Nowadays it seems vital to deeply engage courts and judges in an open and interactive discussion asking the users of justice/citizens whether they are satisfied with the service provided. Not only the volatility of public opinion is well-known,[100] but the advent of social media changed the way 31

---

93 HAGSGARD (2008).
94 PALUMBO et al. (2013).
95 FRIESEN/GEIGER/JORDAN/SULMONETTI (1979).
96 FRIESEN et al. (1979).
97 CHURCH et al. (1978).
98 KRITZER (1979).
99 KRITZER (1979).
100 LANGBROEK (2005).

many stakeholders expect to interact with information,[101] which encompasses producing information on various topics, including justice. Inquiring about the perceptions of the population, when it comes to good justice, will allow the judicial sphere to uncover views that contradict "reality" based on facts and objective indicators (as delays for example). If some studies investigated the importance of cultural aspects in the Judiciary,[102] very few, not to say none especially if we were to focus on Switzerland, ever questioned whether the underlying expectations of judges are aligned with the perceptions of the local/national population. There are examples of research including the views of court users, but they are rather limited to the evaluation of the functioning of the court.[103] This is somehow surprising if we consider that maintaining legitimacy is crucial for courts[104] and that this legitimacy also depends on the way citizens (and other stakeholders) see the judicial institution. For instance, the so-called "Weiser-Erklärung" published in 2007 in Austria, as an ethical code of conduct for judges, put emphasis on the way judicial work is perceived by the population, and on the capacity of judges to continuously analyse and improve their practice.[105] The Council of Europe confirms this view by considering citizens as judicial actors who should be involved in the administration of justice.[106]

32 To summarize, we argue that court culture may be better understood when adopting a macro-institutional perspective, instead of a more classical micro-organisational perspective. It is thus crucial to consider and analyse the expectations of internal actors of the tribunals: judges and non-legal practitioners such as court managers, but also the perceptions of an external actor such as the general public. For the present paper, we have asked citizens of Switzerland to value expectations that have been mentioned during our interviews by various judicial actors of the Swiss Judiciary (see 4).

---

101 WALLACE (2013).

102 CHURCH/LEE/TAN/CARLSON/MCCONNELL (1978), CHURCH et al. (1978), CHURCH (1982), OSTROM et al. (2005), OSTROM et al. (2007).

103 CONTINI/MOHR (2007), HAGSGARD (2008).

104 EICHER/SCHEDLER (2012).

105 TITZ (2011).

106 PAULIAT (2005).

4. Methodology

33 This research seeks to clarify whether and to which extent the expectations of "good justice" differ between judges without any managerial experience and court managers. In a second step it will analyse how these expectations are perceived by the Swiss citizens, and finally to what extent these expectations are management-oriented.

34 At this stage of the research, we decided to focus on dominant expectations and will investigate their underlying values further on. In this regard, expectations are considered as proxies of values.[107] Our approach is inspired by the perceived-value fit but we will investigate the congruence of the perceptions of good justice between Swiss citizens on the one hand and the expectations of internal actors (judges and court managers) on the other, whereas for instance, Vigoda-Gadot and Meiri[108] tested the match of public agents' values with the ones of their own organisation.[109] The choice to focus at this point in time on the citizens as external actors has been dictated by the opportunity to take part in a large quantitative survey addressed to Swiss citizens. We will obviously consider other external stakeholders further on.

4.1 Interviews and sample

35 This research is part of a larger project involving 81 semi-structured interviews in 9 cantons[110] in the three linguistic regions of the nation, with both internal (judges, clerks, court managers, general secretaries, attorneys) and external actors (politicians, lawyers, journalists and researchers) of the courts. The interviewed[111] participants described and defined the qualities necessary for "good justice", and whether they think there is a plurality of role expectations from the main stakeholders to be considered. The aim was to identify and classify dominant expectations, which influence the work of the Judiciary, and more generally, how participants believed the courts are and/or should be managed to produce "good justice".

---

107 HITLIN/PILLIAVIN (2004).
108 VIGODA-GADOT/MEIRI (2008).
109 This comparison will be tested later in the research project using a quantitative approach.
110 Fribourg, Vaud, Luzern, Valais, Jura, Neuchâtel, Ticino, Schaffhausen, Geneva.
111 See appendix 1 for the interview guide.

36 During this exploratory phase, we contacted each secretary general of the judicial organisations surveyed and asked him/her to provide us with a list of interested internal actors with dissimilar profiles (background, gender, job tenure), in order to maximize the diversity of the sample. We specified that we were looking for actors with and without managerial responsibilities, working in different instances (first or second),[112] and in various areas of the justice system (civil, criminal, administrative, public prosecutor's office). As for the external actors, we found them most of the time on the internet and contacted them by phone before meeting with them face to face.

37 For the present paper, we analysed 18 in-depths interviews of court managers (7) and judges without any managerial experience (11) from 10 Swiss courts, in the three linguistic parts of the country. After the completion of the interviews, we manually transcribed the audio recordings. We then analysed them with the NVivo 10 software to identify the main expectations that came out from the statements of the various participants, following the content analysis methodology.[113] According to the inductive methodology and the qualitative saturation technique[114] that we used, we are confident that the final sample represents a sufficiently wide range of situations to accurately grasp what "good justice" means in Switzerland. The idea behind this methodology is to uncover a phenomenon and does not pretend to be necessarily representative.

38 To the contrary, the perception[115] of the Judiciary by Swiss citizens was based on a large representative survey[116] conducted in all cantons of

---

112 The third instance (Supreme Court) will be the subject of another dissertation.

113 Subsequently, we classified interview sections (phrases or entire paragraphs) in 27 different 'knots'. Each knot corresponds to one argument that was individualised as important for 'good justice' by a respondent. Some expectations formulated by one participant can be competing or complementary, as the interviewees were asked to describe how 'good justice' should be according to them first, and then what they believed these expectations were for the other stakeholders. An interviewee could obviously mention several arguments, but one argument mentioned several times by the same respondent was counted only once. Since the amount of interviews was somehow modest, we believed that a classification in three different groups of frequency (see Table 2) was sufficient. STRAUSS/CORBIN (2004).

114 MARTINEAU (2005).

115 As justice expectations of citizens were not available, we used the proxy of justice perceptions, being conscious that the perceptions don't indicate how important each of the perceived dimensions actually is for the citizens.

the country by another group of the national project. In order to define the right questions and to suggest relevant multiple answers to accompany them, we first had a brainstorming among the members of the research team.[117] We based our discussions on the outcome of our exploratory interviews and the results of other similar studies that investigated the judicial sphere by questioning the population.[118] We then tested the questions and their possible answers on a reduced sample of twenty persons composed by other researchers and external people. After the inclusion of those persons' remarks, the research team came back together to produce the final version, which has been translated into the three national languages according to the back translation concept by native speaking persons. In the end the questions were:

- What is your current perception of justice in Switzerland? 17 adjectives[119] were proposed to participants from every canton of Switzerland to answer this question.
- Globally, the image I have of justice is...

Currently, we are unfortunately not able to produce time series data, 39
which would have been interesting to put our results[120] into perspective, as the questionnaire submitted to the population was a "one shot" process only, and there exists no comparable research using the same adjectives as

---

[116] Representative survey (random method) of 3484 persons aged 18 to 74 years, living in Switzerland and using at least once a week the internet. The same questionnaire was used in every canton in the three linguistic regions. At least 100 answers were attained in every canton, and at least 200 in the most densely populated ones. The survey was performed by telephone from March 8th to April 9th 2013 with a confidence interval of 95% and an error margin of 1.7%. 2498 persons answered the questions concerning the Judiciary properly.

[117] The research team was composed by the authors of this contribution and another researcher who works in the Swiss Judiciary.

[118] TOHARIA (2005), SELIGSON/BAVISKAR (2006), GFK SIGNIFICANT (2010).

[119] See table 4 for the complete list of results. These adjectives have been inspired by our interviewees (judges as well as court managers). As the qualitative analysis of all expectations was not achieved at the time of the survey, these adjectives only partially cover those mentioned in paragraph 5.1.

[120] The results of this questionnaire have been treated with the statistical software SPSS 21. In this paper, only descriptive statistics will be presented. Explanatory factor analysis and significant differences between the linguistic regions, as well as between internal and external stakeholders of the Judiciary, will be tested at a later stage, when we will use a quantitative methodology.

ours. In terms of measuring instrument, we decided to use the average[121] since the obtained results are close enough to the median,[122] meaning the impact of extreme values is not substantial on the average.

40 Finally, to analyse the management-orientation of these expectations, we used the theoretical approach developed by Boltanski & Thévenot[123] who classified the reference worlds to which people relate when they justify their actions in collective contexts (see below). This typology is very popular in the French-speaking countries and has been frequently used to analyse values and legitimacy-discourses of (public) sector organisations.[124]

---

[121] An average above 3 on a five-point Likert scale means people agree more than they disagree with the proposed attribute.

[122] The interested reader will find the median results in table 4.

[123] See also the English translation: Boltanski/Thévenot (2006).

[124] Emery/Wyser/Martin/Sanchez (2008).

	Industrial world	**Civic world**	**Commercial/business world**	**Domestic world**
Higher common principle	*Efficiency and "functional" performance*	*Representative collective bodies*	*Competition and market value*	*Personal relationships, hierarchy, tradition*
Succinct presentation of each world	*Inspired by machines, the industrial world places functional performance, professionalism, appropriate action and perfecting resources at the heart of its legitimacy*	*Expression of democratic action, legitimised by legislation, the civic world is based on the emblematic figure of the citizen*	*Competition mechanisms surrounding potential "clients" and profitability are the central themes of the commercial world*	*Inspired by the family, the domestic world reflect benevolent relationships that animate a collective entity, a milieu, a community*
Typical organisational form	*Plant*	*Public sector organization*	*Enterprise*	*Tribe*

Table 1: (Main) reference worlds inspired by Boltanski & Thévenot (1991)

NPM-inspired reforms have been analysed by several scholars as a di- 41
rect confrontation between the civic world (the classical Weberian administration) and the commercial/business world, the latter being supported by management initiatives.[125] This classification will help us determine the spheres of legitimisation to which judges and court managers appeal when they express what "good justice" means for them.

[125] GIAUQUE/CARON (2005), MEYER/HAMMERSCHMID (2006), RONDEAUX (2011).

5. Results and discussion

5.1 Items relating to "good justice" as mentioned by judges without managerial experience, and by court managers

The following table (2) gives an overview of the main expectations mentioned by our interviewees, classified by decreasing frequency:

+++: very frequently mentioned (by at least two-thirds of the interviewees)
++: frequently mentioned (by more than 1/4 of the interviewees)
+: mentioned by one or two interviewees
N=18

	Main expectations related to *good justice*	Expectations of judges	Expectations of court managers
1	**Fast** Justice must solve problems as quickly as possible in order to avoid troubles to the parties due to lengthy procedures. This is what people call the "celerity" of justice.	+++	+++
2	**Client-oriented** Justice is a public service whose aim is to satisfy the needs of the citizens.	+++	+++
3	**Open to the public and the media** Justice has to explain what she does to the public in a comprehensible manner via the media.	++	+++
4	**Independent** Justice has to be independent from any kind of political pressure.	++	++
5	**Transparent** Justice must be transparent when it comes to the way it works. Hiding things to the citizens is not conceivable anymore.	++	++
6	**Humane** Justice is not simply the application of the law. It has to carefully take into account that its raw material is human beings and it may have heavy consequences on their lives.	++	
7	**Close to the people** Justice must be close to the citizens it serves. It must try to understand what the "man of street" lives when it deals with him. This is the idea of a "street-level" justice.	++	+

	Main expectations related to *good justice*	Expectations of judges	Expectations of court managers
8	**Personalised** Justice should consider as much as possible the particularities of every case and situation. It can't apply the same "one size fits all" solution to all cases.	++	
9	**Receptive** Justice must be receptive to what the citizens expect from it. It must have its ear open and listen to the requirements addressed to it.	++	
10	**Fair** Justice has to be fair both in the way it functions and in the manner it renders judgements.	+	
11	**Not too formalistic** Justice shouldn't be too fussy on the rules. It should apply a flexible system that allows it to adapt procedures when necessary.	+	+
12	**Non-jurists, lay people, render judgements** Even the "man of the street" should be permitted to render justice as it represents the "will of the people" as much as jurists do.	+	+
13	**Accountable** Justice in its ivory tower is not acceptable. It is accountable towards society for both its judicial work and for the way it spends the money the State allocates to its functioning.	+	++
14	**Respectful of the procedures** Procedures must be closely followed in every situation.	+	+
15	**Efficient** Justice must use its resources with parsimony and take the most out of them.	+	++
16	**Impartial** Justice has to be freed from any kind of pressures from the parties. It has to judge everyone with the same lenses.	+	
17	**Look for arbitration** Justice should try to reconcile the parties instead of favouring trials.	+	
18	**Global quality** A good quality justice is paramount. Attributes such as fairness, celerity and impartiality are parts of it.	+	+
19	**Treatment fairness** Justice must treat all citizens in an equal mode.	+	

	Main expectations related to *good justice*	Expectations of judges	Expectations of court managers
20	**Pragmatic** A "smart" justice is needed. It has to adapt itself to the various situations it encounters in order to produce the best result.		++
21	**Close to people (geographically)** Courts should be located as closely to people as possible.		++
22	**Efficacy** Justice has to reach objectives and must be able to improve its effectiveness.		++
23	**Inspiring confidence** The whole institution of justice must inspire confidence and must be perceived as reliable by the citizens and parties.		++
24	**Easily accessible** Access to justice must be easy, without any barriers.		+
25	**Not corrupted** Justice has to be freed from any sort of corruption.		+
26	**Affordable (not too expensive)** The cost related to any procedures must be as low as possible (for the parties).		+
27	**Solve all conflicts, all cases** Justice should try to solve any kind of conflicts, should give a clear answer to every situation.		+

Table 2: Main expectations related to "good justice" based on 18 interviews with court managers (7) and judges (11).

42 A careful analysis of the transcripts showed the issue that is the most frequently quoted by judges as well as by court managers is the one of celerity. Certain participants told us they even "prefer a quicker decision rather than a better one at a later point in time". The second most quoted item by both actors is the notion of justice as a public service oriented towards clients (mentioned very frequently, by at least two-thirds of the interviewees). Talking about this argument one judge said: "Yes, we are here to serve the citizens. We are at the disposal of the population, I see the Judiciary as a sort of service".

43 Afterwards, we have a group of arguments mentioned frequently by interviewees (between one quarter and half of them) composed by open to the public and the media, independent, and transparent. Both internal ac-

tors share these five expectations. For example, a court manager told us "the Judiciary is expected to be accountable. We have Public Relations Managers, yearly published reports, information diffused on the internet to explain what we do etc. Justice must live with its time, it is more important to be oriented towards the population than towards the media. It's a question of image for justice that renders it more credible… now we are better perceived".

Overall, without considering the frequency of expectations; about half of them (12 out of 27) are mentioned by court managers and judges. Except the issue of the independence of justice, which is the most frequently quoted when it comes to managerial initiatives within the Judiciary,[126] the four remaining items give the image of a modern public service, customer-oriented and fast, a picture which would perfectly describe agencies managed according to NPM principles.[127] In this respect, these features of good justice may be indicators of a judicial culture, which seems to be at least not incompatible with managerial values and initiatives. One judge well illustrated this concept by telling us "we really have to be transparent, fast and good. Being transparent became very important in the last ten years. This means that everybody must have access to justice. We need open hearings and we should not be too formalistic". 44

It is interesting to note that other judges' expectations with (++), not shared with court managers, focus more or less on the human side of justice (humane, personalised, receptive), whereas other court managers' expectations not shared with judges are more related to an efficient functioning of justice (pragmatic, geographically close to people, efficacy, inspiring confidence). According to this second category of expectations, the managerial orientation seems to be more supported by court managers rather than by judges, whose focal point is deeper directed towards humane justice. This argument has been frequently mentioned during the interviews, when judges expressed their apprehension against a strong focus on productivity through workload indicators, an argument also mentioned in the literature.[128] 45

Finally, the last group of statements used to define "good justice" by judges (mentioned by only one or two interviewees), which do not overlap 46

---

[126] LIENHARD/KETTIGER (2009), LIENHARD (2011).
[127] MOSIMANN (2003), POLLITT (2006).
[128] BÖTTCHER (2004).

with those of court managers, are the following: fair, impartial, look for arbitration, and treatment fairness. They are all related to the judicial core process which involves constitutional guaranties[129] and are frequently incorporated in ethical codes. The same expectations for court managers are easily accessible, not corrupted, financially affordable and solve all conflicts, which is a mix of different qualities more or less related to customer-oriented justice (except not corrupted of course). In that sense, these first results are in line with the evaluations of NPM projects conducted in Switzerland, showing that customer-orientation is one of the main consequences of those NPM reforms.[130]

47 We will now classify judges' and court managers' expectations in regards to "good justice" according to the worlds of Boltanski & Thévenot.[131] As shown in table 3, the world that embraces the majority of expectations from the two groups is the civic one, which is the traditional world for justice expectations and its underlying values in a democratic environment.

Industrial world	**Civic world**	**Commercial (business) world**	**Domestic world**
Fast	Open to the public and the media	Client-oriented	Humane
Efficient	Independent	Not too formalistic	Close to the people
Quality	Transparent	Close to people (geogr.)	Look for arbitration
	Fair	Efficacy	Inspiring confidence
	Non-jurists render judgments	Easily accessible	
	Accountable	Financially affordable	
	Impartial	Personalised	
	Respectful of the procedures	Receptive	
	Treatment fairness	Solve all conflicts all cases	
	Not corrupted		

Table 3: Classification of judges' and court managers' expectations according to the worlds of Boltanski & Thévenot

48 One would indeed expect to find the civic world as the dominant one when it comes to good justice, as it is representative of collective bodies and

129 TOPHINKE (2013).
130 GIAUQUE/ EMERY (2008), RITZ (2003).
131 BOLTANSKI/THÉVENOT (1991).

is based on the figure of the citizen. Nevertheless, these results are not in line with those of a similar research conducted in Switzerland some years ago, based on the same typology of worlds but in a different context.[132] The dominant world was the industrial one, followed by the civic and the domestic worlds. It is therefore very interesting to note that the dominant worlds of reference of court managers and judges are civic and commercial, almost well-balanced. In this kind of hybrid culture, which is archetypical for what is called the post-bureaucratic environment,[133] one of the core problems is to effectively combine the civic and commercial orientations to avoid the juxtaposition of contradictory values. Therefore, the so-called conventions[134] at the basis of any institution,[135] which may be used by internal actors to sublimate the potential conflicts between these two logics and should be the result of a negotiation process where judges are supposed to accept, at least partly, other actors' expectations, will be decisive for a successful reform agenda of the Judiciary. The same proposition is also expressed by many authors dealing with court culture, who emphasise the importance of a shared vision about what "good justice" means.[136]

49 Nonetheless, the two expectations most frequently mentioned by judges and court managers (fast and client-oriented) relate respectively to the industrial and commercial worlds. This is not insignificant if we consider that the majority of values embedded in NPM indeed relate to those worlds as well. This tends to confirm the idea that a new managerial logic may potentially affect the Judiciary as expressed earlier in the paper. Considering the idea that people put an increasing emphasis on their professional values relatively to the more traditional ones to define their culture,[137] and that judges' professional culture represents a crucial part of their identity,[138] we may argue that the boundaries between the various reference worlds will probably fade in order to integrate values from other universes. If this doesn't mean that traditional values will be abandoned it suggests that classical values of the Judiciary, inspired by the civic world, might be potentially colonized by more private sector-oriented expecta-

---

132 EMERY et al. (2008).
133 EMERY (2013), OLSEN (2006).
134 BOLTANSKI/THÉVENOT (1991).
135 DOUGLAS, 1986 quoted in POWELL & DIMAGGIO (1991).
136 LANGER (1994).
137 MORGAN (1989).
138 BOUCKAERT (2007).

tions originating from the industrial and commercial worlds, as the public values would not be in total adequacy with the current society anymore.[139]

50 Additionally, if we recognize that the impact of court organisation on the reputation of the Judiciary has been reinforced,[140] the importance of the industrial and commercial worlds go without saying. Still, the importance of the civic world prevents governments to focus on the economical angle only.[141] Additionally, two trends may reconcile those three worlds and lead to their "hybridisation": the blurring boundaries between administration and judicial work,[142] and the idea that public ethos guarantees that administrative acts are performed embedding values such as equity, ethics and justice.[143]

51 The last world that emerges in this analysis is the domestic one. In this universe, the main principle is based on personal relationships that animate a collective body. Notions that are central to the population such as humanity are found here. It is not by coincidence that this world is the one where we find the majority of expectations from judges after the civic one, as the underlying image of a "caring justice" has often been mentioned. According to an experienced judge: "we should render justice without using any legal argument, without any judicial procedure…"

5.2 Items relating to justice as perceived by the Swiss citizens

52 How do citizens perceive justice nowadays in Switzerland? In particular, are the main expectations of judges and court managers positively perceived by citizens? These are the queries we wanted to solve through a representative survey conducted in all cantons of Switzerland. The 2498 respondents who answered the first question were asked to express to which degree they believed each adjective properly defined justice in Switzerland (on a five-point Likert scale from 1 to 5, 1 being "strongly disagree" and 5 "strongly agree").[144] Table 4 summarizes the results.

---

139 GIAUQUE/ EMERY (2008), EMERY /GIAUQUE (2012).
140 LANGBROEK (2011).
141 LANGBROEK (2005).
142 POLTIER (2012/3).
143 CHANLAT (2003), DU GAY (2005), DU GAY (2009).
144 1 = strongly disagree, 2 = rather disagree, 3 = neither agree nor disagree, 4 = rather agree, 5 = strongly agree. Methodological note: negative arguments have

Items	N	Minimum	Maximum	Average	Standard deviation	Median
*Not corrupted**	3170	1	5	**4.00**	1.05	4
Competent	3248	1	5	**3.79**	0.85	4
Trustworthy	3259	1	5	**3.71**	0.92	4
Independent	3163	1	5	**3.55**	0.97	4
*Not arbitrary** [i]	3128	1	5	**3.51**	1.10	4
Impartial	3216	1	5	**3.39**	1.01	4
Humane	3159	1	5	**3.36**	0.89	3
*Not intimidating** [ii]	3184	1	5	**3.23**	1.13	3
Transparent, open to society	3198	1	5	**3.18**	0.98	3
Efficient, well organised	3134	1	5	**3.16**	1.00	3
Not severe*	3183	1	5	**3.13**	1.04	3
Good communicator	3126	1	5	**3.10**	0.94	3
Understandable (legal procedure for the citizen) [iii]	3145	1	5	**2.93**	1.02	3
Financially affordable	2970	1	5	**2.87**	1.10	3
Self critical	3046	1	5	**2.73**	0.92	3
Fast	3206	1	5	**2.34**	0.98	2
*Not formalistic**	3015	1	5	**2.30**	0.89	2
Valid N (listwise)	**2498**					

Table 4: descriptive statistics of current perception of justice by Swiss citizens

Legend:
1 = strongly disagree / 2 = rather disagree / 3 = neither agree nor disagree / 4 = rather agree / 5 = strongly agree
****= reversed item***
In bold: key expectations of judges and court managers
Underlined: further important expectations of judges
Grey framed: further important expectations of court managers
In italic: other mentioned expectations (by judges as well as by court managers)
Lower-right edged: expectations mentioned neither by judges nor by court managers
i Considered as equivalent of "treatment fairness"
ii Considered as equivalent of "easily accessible"
iii Considered as equivalent of "transparent"

been reversed in order to be comparable with the others. They appear with * in table 4.

53 Among the proposed arguments, the one with which the Swiss population agrees the most to define justice is “not corrupted” (mean: 4), closely followed by “competent” (3.79) and “trustworthy” (3.71), three flattering adjectives in line with the common perception of justice in Switzerland. The other propositions that received an average grade above 3 are “not arbitrary”, “impartial”, “humane”, “not intimidating”, “transparent”, “efficient”, “not severe” and “good communicator".

54 The second question asked to the population was: “Globally, the image I have of justice is…” Again, the interviewees have been given five choices to answer it.[145] Similarly, the result[146] confirms the impression the Swiss citizens have a relatively good opinion of their own justice system.[147] Studies in other countries with comparable judicial systems produced mixed results. We found only a few examples in the scarce literature on the topic: in the Netherlands, research found that confidence in the Judiciary declined at the end of the nineties, while it remained stable around 60% between 2000 and 2005.[148] In Spain, it seems that the situation is improving but the opinion about the functioning of the Judiciary remains mostly negative.[149] Finally, Belgians are 61% to trust their justice, 79% believe that trials are fair and 56% are satisfied with the way justice functions, but they are only 27% to acknowledge that the Judiciary provide enough information on how it works.[150] When it comes to supranational institutions, Europeans are 46% to trust the European Court of Justice,[151] while 72% of Serbians view the International Tribunal for the Former Yugoslavia as very negative or mostly negative.[152]

55 Apart from “not severe”, that we decided to exclude in this first analysis as it is not possible to clearly qualify it as a positive or a negative notion, we can say that all the adjectives that received an above average grade by the population define positively the justice of the country. In other words, Swiss people agree that 11 positive adjectives out of 16

---

145 1=very bad, 2=bad, 3=average, 4=good, 5=very good.

146 Average: 3.63, median: 4, standard deviation: 0.776.

147 Median results were not used as they don’t really diverge from the means, but the interested reader will find them in the tables.

148 Committee for the Evaluation of the Modernisation of the Dutch Judiciary (2006).

149 TOHARIA (2005).

150 GFK SIGNIFICANT (2010).

151 EUROPEAN COMMISSION (2012).

152 OSCE (2009).

properly describe justice. This is quite a high proportion if we consider the scandals that recently appeared in the media (see 2). On the other hand, Swiss citizens believe their justice cannot be defined as "understandable", "financially affordable", "self-critical", "fast" or "not formalistic".

It is now time to turn to the potential fits or misfits between these views of the population and the expectations of court managers and judges without managerial responsibilities analysed in the previous paragraph (5.1). A key issue related to these early observations concerns the notions of a "fast" and "understandable" justice. As seen above, the celerity of the justice system is the number one priority of judges and court managers we interviewed, while it seems that Swiss citizens believe their justice is rather slow. A similar controversy arises when it comes to a comprehensive justice. Magistrates believe that it is one of the most important expectations of the population (despite the fact that the word "comprehensive" has not been used as such), but the citizens perceive their justice as hardly understandable. Those two examples suggest that a clear discrepancy (or misfit) could exist between the perceptions of the population and the expectations of internal actors when it comes to good justice. On the other hand, we saw that those issues are present in the head of judges who underlined the importance to be receptive to the needs of the "customers", that is to say the citizens, in a broader sense. 56

Interestingly, the issue of "not too formalistic", which is indirectly listed in the main expectations, may be in conflict with classical procedural criteria of good justice such as "respectful of the procedures" or even "treatment fairness". These contradictory expectations may lead to some ethical dilemmas as studied by other scholars.[153] 57

According to the population, justice in Switzerland is "impartial", but this notion is only mentioned very rarely as an expectation by judges without managerial experience. The latter probably consider the impartiality of justice as a non-negotiable prerogative already present in the Judiciary and in the judges' ethos. "Efficiency" is also mentioned by judges and court managers, but citizens agree only slightly (3.16) that it defines properly justice in Switzerland. Looking at research conducted on that topic,[154] it is no doubt an essential issue for any good justice. 58

---

153 LUDEWIG/ANGEHRN (2009).

154 KETTIGER (2003), LIENHARD/KETTIGER (2009).

6. Conclusions, limitations and further research

59 In this paper, we analysed the possible differences between the perceptions of the population and the expectations of professional judges without management responsibilities and court managers of the Judiciary around the issue of "good justice". Overall, congruencies seem to be more present than contradictions. Almost half of the expectations are common to both court managers and judges, and the main quoted ones are well compatible with NPM precepts. On the other hand, those expectations shared exclusively by judges relate more to the human side of justice, whereas those specific to court managers focus on how the Judiciary functions, in line with the requirements of their respective professions. As for the perception of the population, it seems that the main discrepancy with the internal actors of the courts relates to the pace justice is rendered, its understandability and its efficiency. In other words, our results suggest that judicial actors are aware that citizens expect a more NPM-oriented institutional culture in the Judiciary, but there is still a long way to get there, legitimizing further reforms.

60 At this stage of the research, some limitations must be considered. First of all, this paper alone does not pretend to uncover the underlying values of the institutional culture of the Judiciary in Switzerland. The expectations and underlying values of other internal and external stakeholders will be considered in the next steps of the project to add to the research. The second problem, which appeared, was the comparison of qualitative with quantitative data. In order to bypass that limitation, we considered the occurrence of the expectations quoted by judges and court managers. In the second part of the paper, we then compared these main expectations with the perceptions of the Swiss population. It would have been very interesting to compare these expectations with those of the population, but such data were (and will so far) unavailable.

61 Another issue is the representativeness of our sample. Although the sample used for the quantitative analysis is representative of the Swiss population, we do not pretend it illustrates the views of all external stakeholders but we believe it is a good estimate and will analyse the opinion of other external actors in subsequent phases of the research. In addition, we are conscious that the sample used for the qualitative part cannot be considered as representative. Nevertheless, we are confident that it is large and varied enough to faithfully depict the idea of "good justice" among the categories of actors surveyed, thanks to an emerging qualitative satu-

ration of arguments.[155] It also goes without saying that having questioned citizens, judges and court managers only once creates a problem in terms of time space. Indeed, it would be valuable to compare the above-mentioned results with others at a later point in time.

It has also to be noted that the interviewers may have induced the large occurrences of the statement regarding justice as a public service, since one question in the interview guide mentioned that argument precisely (see appendix). 62

To conclude, we are convinced that a macro-vision of the Judiciary is required to better understand its culture. Considering the reform agenda of this fundamental institution for any democratic State, the development of a new judicial governance, in the vein of the new public governance proposed by Osborne,[156] would help to better include the various perspectives of both internal and external stakeholders. Nonetheless, it remains that our understanding of the nature and interactions of their respective expectations is still very poor and must be further investigated. 63

7. Appendix

7.1 Interview guide

1) How do you see the changes in courts' managerial and organizational methods in recent years due to the reforms of the Judiciary? 64

2) What are the most important expectations that must be met by the tribunal, particularly as an appeal authority (if applicable)? By which stakeholders (individuals, institutions, professional groups etc.) have these expectations been put forward? Have these expectations evolved in the last ten years? 65

3) What are the expectations that most influence the judge's work today? By which stakeholders (individuals, institutions, professional groups etc.) have these expectations been put forward? Have these expectations evolved in the last ten years? 66

---

155 MARTINEAU (2005).

156 OSBORNE (2006).

67 4) In your opinion, which recent years' reforms have best/worst met the expectations put forward by the tribunal?

68 5) In your opinion, can we talk about a "customer orientation" within the Judiciary in Switzerland today? If yes, who is the "client" of the tribunal? Has this "client" always been the same or has he changed over the last ten years?

69 6) How would you describe in a few words the managerial activity of a court? According to you, who or which body is responsible for the management of the court?

70 7) Who are the tribunal's legal actors and those responsible for management? How would you describe the level of collaboration between the legal actors and those responsible for the management of the tribunal?

71 8) How do you perceive justice management (as a whole) in the tribunal? Is the tribunal well/poorly managed? What do you think are the strengths and what should be improved in the management of the tribunal? (Particularly the assessment of the relationships between steering organs on the one hand, and both steering organs and the General Secretariat on the other, as well as the organization and the structure currently in place).

72 9) How do you think management can contribute to meet the expectations defined in questions 2) and 3)?

73 10) How would you rate judges' acceptance of public management tools (legislative and organizational reforms)? Have you noticed a change in this degree of acceptance during the last ten years?

74 11) What do you think are the main qualities of a "good judge"?

75 12) What do you think are the main qualities of a "good manager "?

76 13) Finally, could you define how "good justice" and a "good tribunal" should look like?

8. Quoted references

Amrani-Mekki, Soraya (2008). Le principe de célérité. Revue française d'administration publique, p. 43-53, vol. 125, no. 1.

Bell, John (2006). Judiciaries within Europe. A comparative review. Cambridge: Cambridge University Press.

Berkson, Larry /Hays, Steven (1977). Applying organization and management theory to the selection of lower court personnel. Criminal Justice Review, p. 81, vol. 2.

Berndt, Thorsten (2010). Richterbilder. Dimensionen richterlicher Selbsttypisierungen. Wiesbaden: Springer.

Bezes, Philippe (2007). Construire des bureaucraties wébériennes à l'ère du new public management? Critique internationale, p. 9-29, vol. 35, no. 2.

Bloor, Geoffrey/Dawson, Patrick (1994). Understanding professional culture in organizational context. Organization Studies, p. 275-295, vol. 15, no. 2.

Boillat, Philippe/Leyenberger, Stéphane (2008). L'administration et l'évaluation du service public de la justice, vu du conseil de l'Europe. Revue française d'administration publique, p. 55-66, vol. 125, no. 1.

Boltanski, Luc/Thévenot, Laurent (1991). De la justification. Les économies de la grandeur. Paris: Gallimard.

Boltanski, Luc/Thévenot, Laurent (2006). On justification: Economies of worth. Princeton University Press.

Böttcher, Hans-Ernst (2004). The role of the judiciary in Germany. German Law Journal, p. 14, vol. 5, no. 10.

Bouckaert, Geert (2007). Cultural characteristics from public management reforms worldwide. In: Schedler, Kuno and Proeller, Isabella (Ed.). Cultural aspects of public management reform. UK: Elsevier.

Brown, Karen J. (2006). Court culture: Measuring and analysing the impact of judicial/administrative culture in the 16th judicial circuit court. Kansas City, Missouri: Institute for Court Management.

Budd, Leslie (2007). Post-bureaucracy and reanimating public governance. A discourse and practice of continuity? International Journal of Public Sector Management, p. 531-547, vol. 20, no. 5.

Burke, Kevin J./Broccolina, Frank (2005). Another view of local legal culture: More than court culture. Court Manager, p. 29-30, vol. 20, no. 4.

Cadiet, Loïc (2011). La théorie du procès et le nouveau management de la justice: Processus et procédure. In: Frydman, Benoît and Jeuland, Eammanuel (Ed.). Le nouveau management de la justice et l'indépendance des juges. Paris: Dalloz.

Cameron, James D./Zimmermann, Isaiah M./Dowling, Mary S. (1987). The chief justice and the court administrator: The evolving relationship. Federal Rules Decisions, p. 439-493, vol. 113.

Canton De Berne (2011). Rapport de gestion 2011 des autorités judiciaires et du ministère public du canton de Berne.

CEPEJ (2014). Rapport sur les "systèmes judiciaires européens – édition 2014 (2012): Efficacité et qualité de la justice". Commission européenne pour l'efficacité de la justice.

Chanlat, Jean-François (2003). L'action publique, l'éthique du bien commun, l'efficacité et l'efficience: Un regard croisé. In: Emery, Yves and Giauque, David (Ed.). Sens et paradoxes de l'emploi public. Lausanne: Presses polythechniques et universitaires romandes.

Church, Thomas W. (1982). Examining local legal culture: Practitioner attitudes in four criminal courts. Washington, DC: National Institute of Justice.

Church, Thomas W. (1985). Examining local legal culture. American Bar Foundation Research Journal, p. 449-518, vol. 10, no. 3.

Church, Thomas W./Carlson, Alan/Lee, Jo-Lynne/Tan, Teresa (1978). Justice delayed: The pace of litigation in urban trial courts. Williamsburg: National Center for State Courts.

Church, Thomas W./Lee, Jo-Lynne/Tan, Teresa/Carlson, Alan/Mcconnell, Virginia (1978). Pretrial delay: A review and bibliography. Williamsburg: National Center for State Courts.

Committee for the Evaluation of the Modernisation of the Dutch Judiciary (2006). Judiciary is quality. The Hague: Committee for the Evaluation of the Modernisation of the Dutch Judiciary.

Contini, Francesco/Mohr, Richard (2007). Reconciling independence and accountability in judicial systems. Utrecht Law Review, p. 26-43, vol. 3, no. 2.

Coolsen, James P. (2008). From the benches and trenches. Case management innovation in a large, urban trial court: The critical importance of legal stakeholder attitudes. The Justice System Journal, p. 70-90, vol. 30, no. 1.

De Santis, Lorenzo G. (2015). Une justice plus commerciale qu'industrielle ? - comparaison des attentes d'une « bonne justice » en Suisse. Canadian Journal of Law and Society / La Revue Canadienne Droit et Société, p. 1-23, First View.

Deal, Terrence E./Kennedy, Allan A. (1982). Corporate cultures : The rites and rituals of corporate life. Addison-Wesley Publishing Compagny.

Delvaux, David (2010). Introduction de compétences managériales dans les cours et tribunaux belges. SociologieS - Dossiers: "L'essor des métiers du conseil : dynamiques et tensions", p. 1-10.

Dewart, Marc/Leroy, Christine (2013). Chef de corps et conseiller en ressources humaines: L'expérience fructueuse d'un binôme. In: Marchandise, Thierry (Ed.). Quel management pour quelle justice? Bruxelles: Larcier.

Douglas, Mary. (1986). How institutions think. Syracuse, N.Y.: Syracuse University Press.

Du Gay, Paul (2005). The values of bureaucracy. Oxford: Oxford University Press.

Du Gay, Paul (2009). Max Weber and the ethics of office. In: Adler, P.S. (Ed.). The Oxford handbook of sociology and organization studies. New York, NJ: Oxford University Press.

Dwivedi, Onkar P./Gow, James I. (1999). From bureaucracy to public management: The administrative culture of the government of Canada. Toronto: Institute of Public Administration & Broadview Press.

Eicher, Angela/Schedler, Kuno (2012). Management responses to multiple rationalities in courts - a review. International Journal For Court Administration, p. 20-34, vol. 4, no. 3.

Eisenstein, James/Flemming, Roy B./Nardulli, Peter F. (1988). The contours of justice: Communities and their courts. New York: University Press of America.

Emery, Yves (2013). Gestion publique des ressources humaines. Introduction. In: Ladner, Andreas/Chappelet, Jean-Loup/Emery, Yves/Knoepfel, Peter/Mader, Luzius/Soguel, Nils and Varone, Frédéric (Ed.). Manuel d'administration publique suisse. Lausanne: Presses polytechniques et universitaires romandes.

Emery, Yves/De Santis, Lorenzo G. (2014). What kind of justice today? Expectations of 'good justice', convergences and divergences between managerial and judicial actors and how they fit within management-oriented values. International Journal For Court Administration, p. 63-75, vol. 6, no. 12.

Emery, Yves/Giauque, David (2012). Motivations et valeurs des agents publics à l'épreuve des réformes. Laval: PUL.

Emery, Yves/Martin, Noemi (2010). Le service public au XXIème siècle. Identités et motivations au sein de l'après-fonctionnariat. Paris: L'Harmattan & Schulthess Editions.

Emery, Yves/Wyser, Carole/Martin, Noemi/Sanchez, Joëlle (2008). Swiss public servants' perceptions of performance in a fast-changing environment. International Review of Administrative Sciences, p. 307-234, vol. 74, no. 2.

European Commission (2012). Public opinion in the European Union – eurobarometer 77 – Spring 2012. European Commission - Directorate-General for Communication.

Fortier, Isabelle/Emery, Yves (2012). L'ethos public en tant que processus social dynamique. Pyramides, p. 83-114, vol. 22, no. 2.

Friesen, Ernest, C./Geiger, Maurice/Jordan, Joseph/Sulmonetti, Alfred (1979). Justice in felony courts: A prescription to control delay, a report on a study of delay in metropolitan courts during 1978-1979. Los Angeles: Whitier College School of Law.

Frydman, Benoît (2011). Le management comme alternative à la procédure. In: Frydman, Benoît and Jeuland, Emmanuel (Ed.). Le nouveau management et l'indépendance des juges. Paris: Dailloz.

Garapon, Antoine (2000). Bien juger. Essai sur le rituel judiciaire. Paris: Odile Jacob.

Gfk Significant (2010). Rapport baromètre de la justice 2010. Belgique: Conseil supérieur de la justice.

Giauque, David (2013). L'administration publique fédérale suisse en comparaison internationale : À la recherche d'une tradition administrative. In: Ladner, Andreas/Chappelet, Jean-Loup/Emery, Yves/Knoepfel, Peter/Mader, Luzius/Soguel, Nils and Varone, Frédéric (Ed.). Manuel d'administration publique suisse. Lausanne: Presses polytechniques et universitaires suisses.

Giauque, David/Caron, Daniel J. (2005). L'identité des agents publics à la croisée des chemins : de nouveaux défis pour les administrations publiques. Contribution au 14ème colloque international de la Revue Politiques et Management Public, Université de Bordeaux.

Giauque, David/Emery, Yves (2008). Repenser la gestion publique. Bilan et perspectives en Suisse. Lausanne: Presses polytechniques et universitaires romandes.

Hagsgård, Marie (2008). Internal and external dialogue: A method for quality court management. International Journal for Court Administration, p. 10-18, vol. 1, no. 2.

Hall, Peter A./Taylor, Rosemary C. (1996). Political science and the three new institutionalisms. Political Studies, p. 936-957, vol. 44, no. 5.

Hamel, Duval J. (2011). La "gestionnarisation" de la justice. In: Frydman, Benoît and Jeuland, Emmanuel (Ed.). Le nouveau management et l'indépendance des juges. Paris: Dalloz.

Hitlin, Steven/Piliavin, Jane A. (2004). Values: Reviving a dormant concept. Annual review of Sociology, p. 359-393, vol. 30.

Hofstede, Geert (1980). Culture's consequences : International differences in work-related values. Beverly Hills: Sage.

Hood, Christopher (1991). A public management for all seasons? Public Administration, p. 3-19, vol. 69, no 1.

Jeuland, Emmanuel (2011). Le renouveau du principe du juge naturel et l'industrialisation de la justice. In: Frydman, Benoît and Jeuland, Emmanuel (Ed.). Le nouveau management de la justice et l'indépendance des juges. Paris: Dailloz.

Kettiger, Daniel (2003). Wirkungsorientierte Verwaltungsführung in der Justiz. Bern: Société suisse des sciences administratives.

Kiener, Regina (2012). Judicial independence in Switzerland. In: Seibert-Fohr, Anja (Ed.). Judicial independence in transition. Heidelberg: Springer.

Kirat, Thierry (2010). Performance-based budgeting and management of judicial courts in France: An assessment. International Journal For Court Administration, p. 12-20, vol. 2, no 2.

Kirkpatrick, Ian/Ackroyd, Stephen/Walker, Richard (2005). The new managerialism and public service professions. Basingstoke: Palgrave McMillan.

Klopfer, Rainer (2007). Vom Richter zum Justizmanager. In: Heer, Marianne and Urwyler, Adrian (Ed.). Justiz und Öffentlichkeit. Bern: Stämpfli.

Kritzer, Herbert M. (1979). Political cultures, trial courts, and criminal cases. In: Nardulli, Peter F. (Ed.). The study of criminal courts: Political perspectives. Cambridge: Ballinger Publishing Company.

Labrusse-Riou, Catherine (2011). Management et statuts d'indépendance: d'un service public - la justice - à d'autres - les hôpitaux et l'université. In: Frydman, Benoît and Jeuland, Emmanuel (Ed.). Le nouveau management et l'indépendance des juges. Paris: Dalloz.

Langbroek, Philip (2005). Quality management concerning judges, judgements and court services. In: Rivero-Cabouat, Noëlle (Ed.). L'administration de la justice en Europe et l'évaluation de sa qualité. Paris: Editions Montchrestien.

Langbroek, Philip (2008). La réorganisation du système judiciaire des Pays-Bas. Revue française d'administration publique, p. 67-79, vol. 125, no. 1.

Langbroek, Philip (2011). Towards a socially responsive judiciary? Judicial independence and accountability in the constitutional contexts of Italy, the USA and Netherlands. In: Frydman, Benoît and Jeuland, Emmanuel (Ed.). Le nouveau management de la justice et l'indépendance des juges. Paris: Dailloz.

Langer, Wolfgang (1994). Staatsanwälte und Richter. Justizielles Entscheidungsverhalten zwischen Sachzwang und lokaler Justizkultur. PhD Thesis. Stuttgart: Bielefeld Universität.

Lienhard, Andreas (2009). Oberaufsicht und Justizmanagement. Justice - Justiz – Giustizia, p. 1-21, vol. no. 1.

Lienhard, Andreas (2011). New Public Management and law: The Swiss case. The NISPAcee Journal of Public Administration and Policy, p. 169-192, vol. 4, no. 2.

Lienhard, Andreas/Bolz, Urs (2001). Staatsrechtliche Kernfragen der wirkungsorientierten Steuerung in den Kantonen. ZBL, p. 1-30.

Lienhard, Andreas/Kettiger, Daniel (2009). Geschäftslastbewirtschaftung bei Gerichten: Methodik, Erfahrungen und Ergebnisse einer Studie bei den kantonalen Verwaltungs und Sozialversicherungsgerichten. ZBL, p. 413-441, vol. 8.

Lienhard, Andreas/Ritz, Adrian/Steiner, Reto/Ladner, Andreas (2005). 10 Jahre New Public Management in der Schweiz. Bilanz, Irrtümer un Erfolgsfaktoren. Bern: Haupt.

Ludewig, Revital (2009). Von der Normalität der richterlichen Arbeitsbelastung - Entscheidungen und Moraldilemmata als Alltag? In: Gass, Stephan/Kiener, Regina/Stadelmann, Thomas/Colliard, Anne/Mosimann, Hans-Jakob and Zappelli, Pierre (Ed.). Justiz ins Blickfeld: Ausgewählte Beiträge aus der Schweizer Richterzeitung 2005-2008. Bern: Weblaw.

Ludewig, Revital/Angehrn, Evelyne (2009). Sind Schöffen noch zeitgemäss? Das Dilemma des modernen Laienrichters zwischen "gesundem Menschenverstand" und rechtlicher Komplexität. Justice - Justiz – Giustizia, p. 32-38, vol. 97, no. 3.

Martineau, Stéphane (2005). L'observation en situation: Enjeux, possibilités et limites. Recherches qualitatives, p. 5-17, Hors Série, no. 2.

Mattijs, Jan (2006). Implications managériales de l'indépendance de la justice. Pyramides, p. 65-102, no 11.

Matz, Adam K./Adams, Julia H./Williamson, Deborah (2011). Understanding culture in Kentucky's courtrooms: An essential tool for management and long-range planning. Juvenile and Family Court Journal, p. 25-42, vol. 62, no. 3.

Meyer, Renate E./Hammerschmid, Gerhard (2006). Public management reform: An identity project. Public Policy and Administration, p. 99-115, vol. 21, no. 1.

Moore, Mark H. (1995). Creating public value. Strategic management in government. Cambridge, Mass.: Harvard University Press.

Morgan, G. (1989). Images de l'organisation. Québec, Canada: Les Presses de l'Université Laval.

Mosimann, Hans-Jakob (2011/1). Leistungsbeurteilung von Richterinnen und Richtern - Qualitätsmerkmal oder Angriff auf die richterliche Unabhängigkeit? Justice - Justiz – Giustizia.

Mosimann, Hans-Jakob (2003). Wege zum Qualitätsmanagement an Gerichten: Grundlagen und Konkretisierung am Beispiel des Sozialversicherungsgerichts des Kantons Zürich. ZBL, p. 470-490.

Olsen, Johan P. (2006). Maybe it is time to rediscover bureaucracy. Journal of Public Administration Research and Theory, p. 1-24, vol. 16, no. 1.

Osborne, Stephen P. (2006). The new public governance? Public Management Review, p. 377-387, vol. 8, no. 3.

Osce (2009). Public perception in Serbia of the ICTY and the national courts dealing with war crimes. Serbia: Organization for Security and Co-operation in Europe.

Ostrom, Brian J./Hanson, Roger A. (1999). Efficiency, timeliness, and quality: A new perspective from nine state criminal trial courts. Williamsburg: National Center for State Courts.

Ostrom, Brian J./Hanson, Roger A./Kleiman, Matthew (2005). Examining court culture. Caseload Highlights, p. 1-6, vol. 11, no. 2.

Ostrom, Brian J./Hanson, Roger A./Ostrom, Charles W./Kleiman, Matthew (2005). Court cultures and their consequences. The Court Manager, p. 14-23, vol. 20, no. 1.

Ostrom, Brian J./Ostrom, C./Hanson, Roger A./Kleiman, Matthew (2005). The mosaic of institutional culture and performance: Trial courts as organizations. Philadelphia: Temple University Press.

Ostrom, Brian J./Ostrom, Charles W./Hanson, Roger A./Kleiman, Matthew (2007). Trial courts as organizations. Philadelphia: Temple University Press.

Palumbo, Giuliana/Giupponi, Giulia/Nunziata, Luca/Mora Sanguinetti, Juan S. (2013). The economics of civil justice: New cross-country data and empirics. OECD Economics Department Working Papers, No. 1060.

Pauliat, Hélène (2005). Les différents modes d'administration de la justice en Europe et au Québec et leur influence sur la qualité. In: Fabri, Marco/Jean, Jean-Paul/Langbroek, Philip/Pauliat, Hélène and Rivero-Cabouat, Noëlle (Ed.). L'administration de la justice en Europe et l'évaluation de sa qualité. Paris: Montchrestien.

Pauliat, Hélène (2007). L'administration de la justice et la qualité des décisions de justice. In: Mbongo, Pascal (Ed.). La qualité des décisions de justice. Poitiers: Editions du Conseil de l'Europe.

Piraux, Alexandre/Bernard, Benoît (2006). Peut-on gérer la justice? Entre responsabilité et indépendance. Pyramides, p. 9-18, vol. 11.

Pollitt, Christopher (2006). Performance management in practice: A comparative study of executive agencies. Journal of Public Administration Research and Theory, p. 25-44, vol. 16, no. 1.

Poltier, Etienne (2011). L'organisation et le fonctionnement interne de l'ordre judiciaire et des tribunaux. Pratique Juridique Actuelle, p. 1017-1036.

Poltier, Etienne (2012/3). Le pouvoir judiciaire s'administre lui-même. Justice - Justiz – Giustizia.

Powell, Walter W./DiMaggio, Paul J. (1991). The new institutionalism in organizational analysis. Chicago: University of Chicago Press.

Ritz, Adrian (2003). Evaluation von New Public Management. Bern: Haupt.

Rondeaux, Giseline (2011). Identification organisationnelle et changement: Le New Public Management à l'épreuve des logiques identitaires, Thèse de Doctorat. Liège: Université de Liège.

Rousseau, Dominique (2011). Exigences constitutionnelles de l'indépendance de la justice et exigences managériales. In: Frydman, Benoît and Jeuland, Emmanuel (Ed.). Le nouveau management de la justice et l'indépendance des juges. Paris: Dalloz.

Schedler, Kuno (2003). Local and regional public management reforms in Switzerland. Public Administration, p. 325-344, vol. 81, no. 2.

Schedler, Kuno/Proeller, Isabella (2007). Public management as a cultural phenomenon. Revitalizing societal culture in international public management research. International Public Management Review, p. 186-194, vol. 8, no. 1.

Schein, Edgar H. (1990). Organizational culture. American Psychologist, p. 109-119, vol. 45, no. 2.

Schmetz, Fernand (2006). Autonomie de gestion des juridictions en Allemagne. Pyramides, p. 145-160, vol. 11.

Seligson, Mitchell A./Baviskar, Siddhartha (2006). 2005 survey of judges in Albania. Arlington, VA: Vanderbilt University.

Serverin, Évelyne (2011). Comment l'esprit du management est venu à l'administration de la justice. In: Frydman, Benoît and Jeuland, Emmanuel (Ed.). Le nouveau management de la justice et l'indépendance des juges. Paris: Dalloz.

Strauss, Anselm/Corbin, Juliet (2004). Les fondements de la recherche qualitative: Techniques et procédures de développement de la théorie enracinée. Fribourg: Academic Press Fribourg.

Stupak, Ronald J. (1991). Court leadership in transition: Fast forward toward the year 2000. The Justice System Journal, p. 617-627, vol. 15, no. 2.

Sugden, Robert (1998). Normative expectations: The simultaneous evolution of institutions and norms. In: Ben-Ner, Avner and Putterman, Louis (Ed.). Economics, values, and organization. Cambridge: Cambridge University Press.

Sullivan, Terasa A./Warren, Elizabeth/Westbrook, Jay L. (1994). The persistence of local legal culture: Twenty years of evidence from the federal bankruptcy courts. Harvard Journal of Law & Public Policy, p. 801-865, vol. 17, no. 3.

Swidler, Ann. (1986). Culture in action: Symbols and strategies. American Sociological Review, p. 273-286, vol. 51.

Thom, Norbert/Ritz, Adrian (2013). Le management public. Concepts innovants dans le secteur public. Lausanne: Presses polytechniques et universitaires romandes.

Titz, Andrea (2011/4). Richterliche Berufsethik - Zeichen echter Unabhängigkeit oder überflüssiger Nabelschau? Justice - Justiz – Giustizia.

Toharia, José Juan (2005). La imagen de la justicia en la sociedad española - noveno barómetro de opinión. España: Consejo General del Poder Judicial.

Tophinke, Esther (2013). Tribunaux et jurisprudence. In: Ladner, Andreas/Chappelet, Jean-Loup/Emery, Yves/Knoepfel, Peter/Mader, Luzius/Soguel, Nils and Varone, Frédéric (Ed.). Manuel d'administration publique suisse. Lausanne: Presses polytechniques et universitaires romandes.

Vauchez, Antoine (2008). Le chiffre dans le "gouvernement" de la justice. Revue française d'administration publique, p. 111-120, vol. 125, no. 1.

Vicentini, J-P. (2011). Le management et l'action du parquet. In: Frydman, B. and Jeuland, E. (Ed.). Le nouveau management de la justice et l'indépendance des juges. Paris: Dalloz.

Vigoda-Gadot, Eran/Meiri, Sagie (2008). New Public Management values and person-organization fit: A socio-psychological approach and empirical examination among public sector personnel. Public Administration, p. 111-131, vol. 86, no. 1.

Vigour, Cécile (2006). Justice : L'introduction d'une rationalité managériale comme euphémisation des enjeux politiques. Droit et Société, p. 425-455, vol. 63, no. 2.

Wallace, Anne. (2013). Courts and social media. Paper presented at the European Group for Public Administration (EGPA), Annual Conference, 11-13 September 2013, Edinburgh, Scotland – UK.

Wipfli, Hans (2006). Justizmanagement am Beispiel eines Steuergerichts: Struktur, Organisation und Führung, Universität Bern: KPM-Verlag.

Zucker, Lynne G. (1991). The role of institutionalization in cultural persistence. In: Powell, Walter P. and DiMaggio, Paul J. (Ed.). The new institutionalism in organizational analysis. Chicago: University of Chicago Press.

Quels freins culturels au management de la justice en Suisse?

Auteurs

Prof. Dr. Yves Emery, Professeur ordinaire, Management public et gestion des ressources humaines, Institut de hautes études en administration publique, Université de Lausanne

Lorenzo Gennaro De Santis, Doctorant FNS, Institut de hautes études en administration publique, Université de Lausanne

Abstract

Ce deuxième chapitre porte sur les freins culturels au management de la justice en Suisse. Il analyse le discours que les acteurs – tout particulièrement les juges- tiennent sur les pratiques de management, les valeurs, représentations, habitudes et manières de penser qui ressortent des quelque 81 entretiens réalisés à cet effet. Après avoir fait un tour de la littérature sur les différentes conceptions de la culture, organisationnelle et institutionnelle, et présenté les principaux arguments sous-tendant le choc potentiel entre culture juridique et managériale, les auteurs développent les nombreux arguments révélés par les entretiens et susceptibles d'expliquer les freins à la managérialisation de la justice. Des arguments liés autant à la spécificité de la justice en général, des tribunaux et du travail des juges et de leur personnalité en particulier, qu'à l'inadéquation supposée des concepts et outils de management au travail de la justice. Il est relevé notamment que les managers, là où ils ont été introduits «ne connaissent ou ne comprennent pas l'activité des juges», et que de toute manière, les juges sont intouchables autant qu'incontrôlables. On mesure alors le chemin qu'il reste à parcourir pour convaincre les juges du bien-fondé des outils de management, et surtout la nécessité d'adapter ceux-ci aux caractéristiques constitutives de l'activité judiciaire.

Sie finden, das [Management] wäre eine niedrigere Kunst, die hohe Kunst ist die Justiz und das rechtliche (...)[1]

(un juge interrogé)

1. Introduction

77 Depuis le début des années 1990, le courant de la nouvelle gestion publique (NGP) a beaucoup influencé les pratiques de management au sein des organisations publiques. En Suisse, quelques publications marquantes ont contribué à diffuser ces méthodes,[2] largement importées du secteur privé, et destinées à améliorer l'efficience et l'efficacité des administrations publiques. Parmi les idées essentielles caractérisant ce mouvement, qui a exercé une forte influence en Suisse,[3] relevons la conduite stratégique, la détermination de contrats ou mandats de prestations attribuant aux managers publics des enveloppes globales pour atteindre les objectifs fixés à leur entité, la délégation de responsabilités permettant une marge de manœuvre élargie dans la conduite opérationnelle, l'orientation client et les systèmes qualité, ainsi que les pratiques de gestion des ressources humaines favorisant la performance et le développement des compétences. Une évolution qui n'a pas manqué d'influencer également les organisations du pouvoir judiciaire, avec un décalage d'une dizaine d'années par rapport aux premières expériences pilotes dans l'administration.[4] Et même si cette influence, comme nous allons le montrer, est demeurée marginale à ce jour, pour des raisons au moins autant techniques (spécificités de l'activité judiciaire) que culturelles (valeurs véhiculées au sein du pouvoir judiciaire), une accélération manifeste peut être constatée depuis quelques années.

78 Wipfli résume différentes initiatives de modernisation de la Justice en Suisse, au niveau fédéral et cantonal.[5] Des initiatives issues en particulier

---

1 « Ils trouvent [les juges] que le management serait un art mineur, l'art majeur est la justice et le juridique… ».

2 DELLEY (1994), BUSCHOR/SCHEDLER (1995).

3 GIAUQUE/ EMERY (2008).

4 KETTIGER (2003).

5 WIPFLI (2006).

du souci de décharger les tribunaux de plus en plus engorgés, en simplifiant les procédures d'accès à la justice, en améliorant les processus de traitement des objets soumis aux Tribunaux, ainsi qu'en simplifiant les voies de recours, comme c'est notamment le cas au niveau fédéral.[6]

Ces préoccupations concernent d'abord la relation entre le justiciable, 79
les avocats et l'appareil judiciaire, moins l'organisation interne et le management des Tribunaux. Dans certains cantons, à l'image de Berne, les principes de la nouvelle gestion publique introduits dans l'administration ont exercé une influence sur le management des organisations du pouvoir judiciaire, qui ont pu tester la méthode et en apprécier le potentiel comme les limites pour contribuer à une «bonne» justice. Mais ces exemples constituent l'exception, l'essentiel des tribunaux suisses étant demeurés à l'écart de telles initiatives. Pourquoi?

A bien des égards, la NGP s'est développée en contre-pied du modèle 80
bureaucratique classique, au fondement du fonctionnement des organisations publiques.[7] Considérant la logique du marché et de l'entreprise privée comme la clé de la résolution des problèmes publics,[8] ce modèle bureaucratique né au début du siècle passé a fait l'objet d'importantes remises en cause depuis une bonne vingtaine d'années, notamment parce qu'au motif d'être fondamentalement démocratique par la légitimité de son action, il a souvent conduit à défendre la règle (ou plus généralement la loi) pour elle-même, en amenant les fonctionnaires à perdre le sens de leur mission et en oubliant de servir les usagers des services publics,[9] un argument servi par analogie au monde de la justice.[10]

Dans ce contexte où l'administration publique est fortement critiquée, 81
la NGP propose un changement de culture qui, d'une nature essentiellement juridique, fondée sur le respect des procédures, la loyauté hiérarchique et la primauté des enjeux d'équité, devrait évoluer vers une culture plus entrepreneuriale, axée sur le leadership des managers publics, la prise de risque, l'orientation vers les résultats, la concurrence et l'attrait du gain comme sources d'innovations managériales.[11] A priori, ces nouvelles

---

6 VOIR PAR EX. BGG, SR 173.110.
7 WEBER (1971).
8 DESMARAIS/JEANNOT/LOUVEL/PERNOT/SAGLIO/UGHETTO (2007).
9 EMERY (2009).
10 LANGBROEK (2005).
11 DENHARDT/ DENHARDT (2003).

orientations ne sont pas exactement celles que l'on choisirait pour qualifier le fonctionnement des tribunaux, ce qui pose la question fondamentale de leur compatibilité avec les principes régissant le pouvoir judiciaire.

82 Ce chapitre a pour objectif d'analyser les motifs culturels, liés aux valeurs, représentations, habitudes et manières de penser présentes au sein du pouvoir judiciaire, comme l'une des explications privilégiées pour comprendre ce que nous pourrions appeler la résistance à la managérialisation du pouvoir judiciaire. Aussi, la question de recherche traitée est la suivante: Quels sont les motifs ressortant de la culture du pouvoir judiciaire d'une manière générale, et des juges en particulier, susceptibles d'expliquer l'introduction différée des principes de nouvelle gestion publique au sein des tribunaux?

83 Après avoir résumé la littérature pertinente sur cette question, nous allons présenter les arguments essentiels évoqués par les principaux acteurs de la justice lors d'un programme d'interviews réalisés durant les années 2012-2013, afin d'en extraire les motifs pouvant être associés à la culture du pouvoir judiciaire. Il sera pour cela nécessaire de définir préalablement ce que nous entendons par culture comme attribut institutionnel et organisationnel, pour montrer ensuite les principales réflexions liées à la culture du pouvoir judiciaire, et son éventuelle compatibilité avec la culture véhiculée par le mouvement de la NGP.

84 La réceptivité que la justice en général, et les tribunaux plus spécifiquement, montrent aux valeurs et méthodes de management, peut être analysée sous deux angles essentiellement. Le premier, qui ne fera pas l'objet de ce chapitre, est représenté par une approche technique et objective de la compatibilité des approches de management aux actes juridiques et aux processus au cœur de l'activité judiciaire. On peut ainsi arguer du fait que l'activité qui consiste à «dire le droit», sur la base des lois et de la jurisprudence, ainsi que des règles de procédures en vigueur, en gérant un flux de dossiers entrants par définition incontrôlable, ne se prête guère à l'introduction de techniques de management développées avant tout dans le monde industriel.[12] Cet auteur montre notamment que la difficulté à évaluer l'efficacité de la justice oriente les contrôles plutôt vers l'efficience de son fonctionnement, l'assimilant à une chaîne de production calquée sur l'entreprise. Mais l'autonomie des magistrats, l'absence d'autonomie financière des tribunaux ainsi que la faiblesse des pouvoirs

---

12 AMADIEU (2012).

détenus par le président du tribunal sur les juges, sont quelques caractéristiques parmi beaucoup d'autres qui limitent singulièrement l'application des méthodes de management à la justice.

L'autre approche, développée dans ce chapitre, aborde la question sous l'angle plus difficilement perceptible de la *culture* du pouvoir judiciaire. 85
En effet, il a été maintes fois démontré que l'introduction de nouvelles méthodes de fonctionnement dans les organisations est avant tout un défi culturel, en ce sens que les valeurs, représentations et habitudes des membres de l'organisation se trouvent remises en question par ces changements. La culture propre aux organisations, souvent baptisée de manière générique «culture d'entreprise» a, dès le début des études réalisées au sein des organisations, été mise en évidence comme l'un des facteurs-clés de succès ou d'échec de tout changement organisationnel, [13] au-delà des difficultés fonctionnelles ou techniques que l'organisation peut rencontrer.

2. Revue de littérature

2.1 Différentes compréhensions de la culture au sein du pouvoir judiciaire

Il est bon de rappeler ici que si la dimension culturelle des organisations a toujours existé, elle n'a été conceptualisée en tant que variable 86
essentielle dans le management qu'au début du XXème siècle, en particulier avec les travaux de l'équipe de E. Mayo.[14] Il faut attendre toutefois les années 1970-80 pour assister à une reconnaissance de l'importance de la variable culturelle dans la littérature du management.[15] Aujourd'hui, dans les organisations publiques, la dimension culturelle est principalement abordée à travers les questions relatives aux valeurs caractéristiques du secteur public et à l'ethos public, c'est-à-dire davantage au niveau institutionnel qu'organisationnel.[16] Cela dit, les évaluations liées à l'introduction de la NGP dans les administrations publiques, en Suisse comme ailleurs, ont montré que cette nouvelle méthode de gestion avait été considérée comme une approche technique avant tout, alors qu'elle véhiculait de

---

13 PÜMPIN/KOBI/WÜTHRICH (1985), JONES/REDMAN (2000), COLLERETTE/SCHNEIDER (2004).
14 MAYO (1933).
15 SCHEIN (1971), DEAL/KENNEDY (1982).
16 PERRY/VANDENABEELE (2008), EMERY /GIAUQUE (2012).

nouvelles valeurs, une nouvelle culture de fonctionnement, voire une nouvelle idéologie,[17] et que cette dimension culturelle avait été largement sous-estimée par les responsables politiques et administratifs en charge de sa mise en œuvre.[18]

87 Si l'on définit la culture appliquée au monde des organisations comme étant *un ensemble de perceptions, de significations et de croyances sur l'organisation, qui facilite l'élaboration du sens au sein d'un groupe d'individus qui partagent une expérience commune, et guide le comportement individuel au travail*[19], la culture apparaît essentielle pour comprendre comment fonctionne n'importe quelle organisation. La culture peut être déclinée à plusieurs niveaux *systémiques,* selon l'angle et le périmètre d'analyse retenus. Ainsi, toute organisation présente une culture et des sous-cultures, illustrant le fait que des domaines d'activité différents s'exercent en son sein, contribuant à façonner des *variations culturelles* qui seront finalement harmonisées sur une tonalité plus générale englobant toute l'organisation.[20] Pour la justice, on peut ici typiquement mentionner les différents domaines du droit (civil, pénal, administratif) comme expression de potentielles sous-cultures au sein de la Justice. De même, toute organisation est présente dans un environnement plus large, une région, voire un pays, qui portent également une culture et influencent les organisations exerçant sur ce territoire.[21] Dans le même registre, les *institutions* caractérisant un système politique et administratif sont porteuses de valeurs qui, peu ou prou, façonnent celles, plus spécifiques, des organisations qui les constituent.[22] Dans ce contexte, les professions représentent une forme d'institution intéressante, en ce qu'elles résultent d'un processus d'élaboration progressive de standards auxquels leurs membres doivent pouvoir répondre pour en faire partie,[23] et qui les protègent ensuite d'éventuels «prétendants» ne présentant pas toutes les qualités requises. Ce qui est notablement le cas pour les juges, au cœur de l'activité judiciaire.

---

[17] Bezes (2003).
[18] Schedler/Proeller (2007).
[19] Bloor/Dawson (1994), p. 276.
[20] Schneider (1990).
[21] Hofstede (1998).
[22] DiMaggio (1991).
[23] Dubar/Tripier (2005).

Partant de ce constat et de la diversité des grilles d'analyse de la dimension culturelle, nous allons retenir ici principalement trois niveaux, étant entendu que la culture nationale n'est a priori pas pertinente puisque l'ensemble des entretiens a été réalisé en Suisse.[24] 88

Le niveau de la culture *institutionnelle*, véhiculant des valeurs spécifiques au pouvoir judiciaire: on peut ici s'interroger sur la compatibilité entre les valeurs institutionnelles de la justice, ancrées notamment dans la Constitution, et celles portées par la NGP. La mission confiée au pouvoir judiciaire, l'indépendance caractérisant son fonctionnement, et l'importance d'établir la vérité, plus que des considérations d'efficacité ou d'efficience, dominent le fonctionnement du judiciaire et peuvent représenter un frein à la managérialisation du troisième pouvoir. Incontestablement, le pouvoir judiciaire exerce un rôle déterminant pour légitimer l'Etat de droit dans les sociétés démocratiques. Avec Vigour, relevons que «L'institution judiciaire est conçue comme une institution productrice de valeurs et de symboles […], elle se présente hors du temps et hors du monde».[25] Ces caractéristiques institutionnelles du pouvoir judiciaire pourraient même conduire à une forme de *culture «judiciaire»* très particulière, présentant des traits spécifiques et partagés le distinguant d'autres institutions du secteur public, en particulier les administrations, par analogie à la notion de *culture administrative* développée par certains auteurs.[26] C'est une idée qui se rapproche de la notion de *local legal culture*,[27] même si cette dernière par sa conception même est plus localisée que l'institution judiciaire dans son ensemble. 89

Le niveau de la culture *organisationnelle*. Aujourd'hui, les organisations du pouvoir judiciaire, les tribunaux, doivent composer avec une pression nouvelle liée à plusieurs facteurs, en partie communs à ceux qui s'exercent sur les organisations publiques en général: gestion plus serrée des ressources, voire restrictions budgétaires, transparence accrue attendue de la part des parties prenantes, exigences de qualité liées aux prestations fournies, contrôle de performance et imputabilité face aux instances de contrôle (le conseil supérieur de la magistrature ou d'autres instances 90

[24] Les clivages linguistiques, ville/campagne, etc., à l'intérieur de la Suisse, pourraient avoir un impact intéressant à analyser, mais la présente étude n'a pas intégré cette dimension.

[25] VIGOUR (2008).

[26] EMERY (2010).

[27] CHURCH (1985).

politiques en charge de la haute surveillance de la justice).[28] Cette pression grandissante conduit à ce que nous appellerions une «banalisation» de la justice, conçue comme une organisation productive, intégrée dans une chaîne de production plus large qui inclut le ministère public, les forces de police et les institutions en charge de l'exécution des peines. Pour ce faire, les organisations du pouvoir judiciaire au plan international mettent sur pied des systèmes de controlling, d'optimisation de la charge de travail, des enquêtes auprès de leurs «clients», voire des systèmes intégrés exploitant les différents outils de la NGP, en partant de l'idée que les tribunaux constituent des *entreprises* de service.[29] La création de fonctions de secrétaires généraux rattachés à la présidence des tribunaux, de directeurs de l'administration ou encore de *managers de la justice*[30], témoigne de cette préoccupation nouvelle d'optimisation du fonctionnement organisationnel de la justice. Une préoccupation qui est portée au niveau international par différentes institutions travaillant à l'efficacité et à la qualité des organisations du pouvoir judiciaire, en particulier la Commission européenne pour l'efficacité de la justice (CEPEJ),[31] qui développe un système de qualité pour les tribunaux et un ensemble d'indicateurs de gestion permettant d'apprécier les différentes facettes de leur fonctionnement.[32] Ce dispositif est d'ailleurs appliqué également en Suisse au niveau du Tribunal fédéral. Les spécialistes de la culture organisationnelle montrent que celle-ci ne peut être transformée qu'au terme d'une démarche de longue haleine qui mobilise les processus de socialisation et d'invention de la réalité caractérisant les organisations appréhendées comme construits sociaux. Pour Bloor/Dawson[33] qui soutiennent cette approche avec la majorité des spécialistes de la culture organisationnelle, la culture est historiquement et socialement construite en tant qu'attribut global de l'organisation, et est par conséquent difficile à changer. Dans cette conception, la culture contribue à donner du sens et à interpréter la réalité que vivent les membres de l'organisation, à travers des schèmes cognitifs communs, des valeurs et des normes qui vont influencer le comportement au travail. Cette variable culturelle en tant qu'attribut de l'organisation sera d'autant plus prégnante que l'institution analysée présente des spéci-

28 POLTIER (2012).
29 LIENHARD (2009).
30 WIPFLI (2006).
31 CEPEJ (2014).
32 CEPEJ (2010).
33 BLOOR/DAWSON (1994).

ficités qui la distinguent d'autres organisations, et qu'elle dispose d'une autonomie forte, ce qui est le cas des organisations du pouvoir judiciaire.

Finalement, le niveau de la culture *professionnelle* des acteurs au centre du pouvoir judiciaire, à savoir les juges. La managérialisation des organisations publiques a été analysée par de nombreux auteurs comme venant contrecarrer des valeurs et logiques d'action professionnelles qui, dans la conception wébérienne de l'administration, représentent le cœur de leur légitimité et de leur fonctionnement.[34] Les professionnels vont alors exploiter leurs marges de manœuvre pour légitimer leurs systèmes de valeurs comme noyau culturel dominant.[35] Un phénomène particulièrement marqué lorsque l'organisation vit un changement en profondeur,[36] tel qu'actuellement à travers le mouvement de *managérialisation* issu de la vague de NGP en Suisse. Les organisations composant le pouvoir judiciaire, qui peuvent être assimilées à une bureaucratie professionnelle au sens de la typologie de Mintzberg,[37] sont portées par les professionnels au centre de leur activité, les juges, représentants d'une profession à la *culture remarquable*.[38] Dans les bureaucraties professionnelles, la culture des professions au cœur de l'activité exercée est souvent dominante et influence l'ensemble du fonctionnement de l'organisation. Il en va ainsi des organisations d'enseignement (écoles, universités), de soins (hôpitaux), mais également de la justice: dans toutes ces organisations, les «opérateurs» fournissant directement les prestations sont des professionnels très qualifiés, souvent portés par des corporations elles-mêmes très actives pour défendre leurs intérêts. Ainsi, la culture professionnelle peut s'inscrire en véritable barrière au développement de la managérialisation, cette dernière étant perçue comme menaçant les logiques professionnelles dominant les modes d'action caractéristiques des juges.[39] 91

La dimension culturelle, qu'elle soit ancrée au niveau institutionnel, organisationnel ou professionnel, constitue une variable essentielle qui façonne le comportement des acteurs-clés du système analysé, la percep- 92

34 EXWORTHY/HALFORD (1999), HALFORD/LEONARD (1999), THOENIG (2000), SEHESTED (2002), KIRKPATRICK/ACKROYD/WALKER (2005), ROUBAN (2007), CARBONI (2008).
35 DOLAN/ROSENBLOOM (2003).
36 BLOOR/DAWSON (1994).
37 MINTZBERG (1982).
38 BOUCKAERT (2007).
39 AMADIEU (2012).

tion et l'analyse de leur «réalité», les options qui s'en dégagent, les comportements estimés acceptables et la manière de juger les réalisations issues de l'action collective.

2.2 Culture juridique et culture managériale: une intégration possible ou un choc programmé?

93 Face aux bilans en demi-teinte des évaluations portant sur la NGP en Suisse,[40] et à l'étranger également,[41] il faut attendre le début du XXIème siècle pour trouver des réflexions mettant en avant la faible prise en compte de la dimension culturelle comme l'une des explications plausibles de ces constats. Typiquement, l'article de Schedler et Proeller souligne combien cette dimension a été sous-estimée dans la mise en œuvre des réformes de type NGP au sein des administrations publiques, réformes comprises essentiellement comme l'introduction de méthodes de gestion inspirées du management privé.[42] Ce choc culturel n'est a priori pas moins important au sein du pouvoir judiciaire, [43] mais le caractère singulier de cette institution fait penser qu'il risque d'être encore plus marqué que dans les administrations.[44] Il y a longtemps déjà, une des craintes liées à la managérialisation des administrations publiques était résumée par Laufer/Burlaud comme étant l'introduction d'une logique de *mort potentielle* au sein d'institutions perçues comme pérennes,[45] puisque la logique de compétition propre au marché peut amener les entreprises privées à disparaître. Dans le pouvoir judiciaire, c'est moins la menace de mort que la crainte de perdre «l'exceptionnalité» de la justice, selon les termes de Vigour,[46] qui se profile comme l'élément-clé de résistance institutionnelle. Mais d'où vient cette exceptionnalité?

94 Commençons par rappeler les principes fondamentaux autour desquels s'articule la justice et qui influencent sa culture institutionnelle. Selon

---

40 RIEDER/FARAGO (2000), EMERY /GIAUQUE (2003), LEUENBERGER (2005), SCHMIDT (2007), GIAUQUE/EMERY (2008).
41 CHRISTENSEN/LAEGREID/RONESS/ROVIK (2007).
42 SCHEDLER/PROELLER (2007).
43 LIENHARD (2011).
44 HAMEL (2011), MARCHANDISE (2013).
45 LAUFER/BURLAUD (1980).
46 AMADIEU (2012).

Frydman,[47] quatre principes fondamentaux sont à considérer au niveau institutionnel (constitutionnel):

1) l'indépendance du pouvoir judiciaire à l'égard des autres pouvoirs. Pour réussir, le management du troisième pouvoir devrait ainsi être nécessairement une forme «d'auto-management» 95

2) l'indépendance du juge en tant qu'auteur d'un acte juridictionnel. Une indépendance qui peut rendre problématiques les indicateurs utilisés pour évaluer son travail (taux de recours, jugements cassés par l'instance supérieure, productivité, etc.), peu compatibles avec l'ethos professionnel des juges[48] 96

3) la légalité de la procédure. Les règles managériales ne doivent pas aboutir à contourner la procédure voulue par le législateur, ou à en omettre certaines phases. 97

4) l'économie du procès, les règles du procès équitable, où la sécurité du droit, par une décision rapide et définitive, est contrebalancée par une décision juste, guidée par le choix du meilleur argument au terme d'un débat contradictoire. 98

Avec P. Ricoeur et J. Derrida, on relèvera également que l'acte de juger met en jeu une responsabilité infinie, requérant une liberté de jugement totale. Sur cette base, Frydman conclut qu'«il y a donc un travail d'adaptation et d'accommodation du nouveau management aux valeurs du judiciaire qui doit nécessairement être entrepris» (p.88). 99

E. Alt analyse l'emprise du management, vecteur d'une idéologie souvent dissimulée,[49] sur les rapports de pouvoir au sein des tribunaux, en définissant notamment des nouveaux indicateurs de performance.[50] Sur la base d'une présentation d'objectifs et d'indicateurs au sein de différents pays européens, l'auteur critique alors la justice subordonnée à une vision utilitariste, réduite à une production, un service marchand. Dans cette perspective, «L'important n'est pas le procès, mais le process» (p. 95). Il critique aussi la conception du juge comme maillon d'une chaîne de production, juge qui doit développer sa capacité de répondre à des demandes extérieures multiples comme celles du Parquet, de la Police, de l'admini- 100

---

47 Frydman (2013).
48 Vigour (2006), Bernard/Drumaux/Mattijs (2012).
49 Gaulejac De (2005).
50 Alt (2013).

stration pénitentiaire, du ministère de la Justice, etc. Les pratiques de management visant à rationaliser le fonctionnement de la justice, telles que la gestion différenciée des délais selon la complexité des cas (Differentiated Case Management, DCM), sont un bon exemple révélant les résistances et craintes par rapport à un système vu comme transformant la justice en travail à la chaîne standardisé, ne tenant pas compte du caractère unique de chaque cas.[51] Vigour apporte des arguments supplémentaires à la difficile compatibilité des méthodes de management avec les logiques d'action du pouvoir judiciaire,[52] en soulignant également que l'introduction d'une rationalité de type managérial va de pair avec une forme de consumérisme considérant le justiciable comme un «client» auquel l'organisation judiciaire livre des «prestations», évaluées par des enquêtes de «satisfaction». Il s'agit de méthodes qui relèvent d'une approche de type marketing, pour le moins étrangère, pour ne pas dire clairement antinomique, aux valeurs fondant l'institution judiciaire.

101 Pour Frydman, «il y a donc, dans le projet d'introduire la logique managériale dans le cœur même de l'appareil constitutionnellement chargé de veiller à l'application et au respect du droit, quelque chose qui pourrait ressembler à un cheval de Troie et qui contribue à expliquer une certaine hostilité, en tout cas une certaine défiance à l'égard de l'importation de ces normes nouvelles».[53] Pour contrer cela, Alt met en avant «l'éthique de la qualité», selon laquelle des évaluations plurielles et non-chiffrées doivent être utilisées (voir par ex. la check-list de la CEPEJ, 2008). Parmi les critères suggérés, relevons:[54] l'accès à la justice, la célérité du procès, la stabilité et la prévisibilité des jugements, la qualité de la relation entre le juge et les parties, l'intelligibilité des décisions rendues, la possibilité d'en obtenir l'exécution, l'acceptabilité sociale de la justice rendue (légitimité, confiance en la justice), ainsi que l'indépendance et l'impartialité. On mesure à quel point les méthodes souvent réductrices pour évaluer l'activité d'un tribunal, voire celle d'un juge individuel, peinent à révéler la complexité subtile de leur activité.

102 P. Martens va plus loin et recommande une forme «d'annexion du management au droit», puisqu'il s'agit «de construire un management propre au droit plutôt que de se résigner à n'être qu'une peuplade colonisée par

51 Coolsen (2008).
52 Amadieu (2012).
53 Frydman (2013), p. 82.
54 Alt (2013).

lui».[55] Dans l'analyse de ce rapport difficile entre culture judiciaire, ethos professionnel des juges et culture managériale, les scénarios dégagés par Ferlie and Geraghty[56] sont particulièrement intéressants. Selon ces auteurs, plusieurs scénarios sont possibles dans le cadre de la confrontation entre professionnalisation et managérialisation. Les deux premiers scénarios partent de l'idée que la logique managériale prendra *in fine* le dessus. Le premier est une domination du côté management, qui efface les logiques professionnelles: certains auteurs parlent de «détraditionnalisation» de la justice,[57] ou encore de la fin de l'exceptionnalité de la justice, [58] laquelle est obligée de se conformer aux principes et règles du management, qui exercent un contrôle sur la qualité (et la quantité) du travail fourni, en mobilisant un processus de définition des objectifs et de critères d'évaluation visant à maximiser la «performance». Ce qui nous renvoie au débat très actuel sur la performance comparative des tribunaux, voire des juges, y compris du rôle que peut y jouer une culture organisationnelle spécifique.[59] Mais cette tendance traduirait également la fin de l'institution judiciaire placée sur un piédestal la situant en-dessus de la société, et donc des règles d'imputabilité que les citoyens sont en droit d'attendre de toute institution «normale».

La seconde hypothèse est plus nuancée pour mettre en avant une forme 103
de managérialisation douce des tribunaux. Les juges seraient ainsi invités à intégrer une logique et des outils managériaux dans leurs propres pratiques, sans toutefois les révolutionner, mais en développant une nouvelle culture professionnelle hybride, compatible avec les outils de management. Il s'agit d'une tendance que nos travaux ont pu mettre en exergue en Suisse.[60]

Les deux scénarios suivants partent au contraire de l'idée que la culture 104
professionnelle des juges résistera au mouvement de managérialisation. Tout d'abord, le troisième scénario peut être décrit comme la colonisation du management par les juges, lesquels s'approprieraient et transformeraient les nouvelles exigences managériales pour qu'elles demeurent conformes à leurs pratiques habituelles, à leur ethos. Le fait que les tribunaux

---

55 MARTENS (2013), P. 114.
56 FERLIE/GERAGHTY (2007).
57 BERNARD et al. (2012), P. 25.
58 AMADIEU (2012).
59 OSTROM/HANSON/OSTROM/KLEIMAN (2005).
60 EMERY /DE SANTIS (2014).

soient dirigés par des juges et que les non-juristes, même au plus haut niveau, n'exercent dans la présidence des tribunaux ou des cours qu'une voix consultative, peut faire penser que cette troisième option a de bonnes chances de se réaliser. Finalement, le dernier scénario correspond à un renforcement de la logique professionnelle, une forme de *reprofessionnalisation* des tribunaux qui seraient parvenus à contenir le management pour le réduire au rang de phénomène passager, voire de mode. Si les évaluations portant sur les méthodes de management introduites dans les tribunaux devaient se révéler catastrophiques, on peut imaginer une forme de résurgence du pouvoir du juge et de la logique purement professionnelle comme seule légitimité de l'action du pouvoir judiciaire. Un scénario certes peu probable, mais pas dénué d'intérêt.

105 En période de changement, la transformation de la culture est particulièrement importante pour comprendre les avancées ou blocages du processus d'évolution, et constitue un enjeu de pouvoir fort, [61] certains groupes d'acteurs –en particulier des corps professionnels constitués dont l'obédience dépasse les frontières de l'organisation- étant mieux à même de mettre en avant leurs valeurs pour influencer le changement culturel dans la direction qui les avantage le plus. Cette approche *micro-politique* de la dimension culturelle, qui se trouve être d'ailleurs au fondement de certaines définitions de la culture,[62] nous paraît pertinente pour apprécier les transformations que vivent les organisations du pouvoir judiciaire aujourd'hui.

3. Méthode

106 La présente étude s'inscrit dans le cadre d'une recherche approfondie sur la réceptivité culturelle des tribunaux suisses aux outils et méthodes de management. Elle fait partie d'un projet plus large portant sur le management de la justice helvétique[63] conduit au niveau national depuis 2012. Pour ce chapitre, nous avons analysé une série d'entretiens (81) semi-structurés menés dans des tribunaux de première et seconde instance dans des cours civiles, administratives et criminelles de neuf cantons,[64]

---

[61] DOLAN (2000).
[62] DE GAULEJAC/MERCIER (2012).
[63] Voir www.justizforschung.ch.
[64] Les cantons latins (Fribourg, Genève, Jura, Neuchâtel, Tessin, Vaud et Valais) sont l'objet principal de la recherche, pour des raisons linguistiques principale-

dans les trois régions linguistiques du pays. Nous nous sommes entretenus tant avec des acteurs internes au tribunal (juges, greffiers, procureurs, secrétaires généraux et personnel administratif), qu'avec des acteurs externes à la justice (politiciens, avocats, journalistes, académiques), l'idée principale étant de faire ressortir et de croiser le point de vue de ces différents acteurs sur le fonctionnement actuel et les transformations –de nature non strictement juridique- affectant les organisations du pouvoir judiciaire. Ce faisant, les personnes rencontrées étaient amenées à parler de leur vision de la justice et du fonctionnement des tribunaux, révélatrice des éléments constitutifs d'une *bonne* justice ainsi que des menaces et opportunités liées à l'introduction de techniques de management dans le pouvoir judiciaire.

Les interviews, d'une durée d'environ une heure chacun, ont été con- 107
duites selon la méthodologie inductive[65] dans le but d'obtenir une vue d'ensemble des principaux arguments mis en avant par nos interlocuteurs, jusqu'à saturation des arguments.[66] Les enregistrements audio des interviews ont ensuite été retranscrits et codés à l'aide du logiciel NVivo 10 dans le but d'identifier les principaux leviers et freins à l'introduction des nouvelles approches de management dans la justice. Plus de 200 nœuds, basés sur une analyse du contenu des discours des personnes rencontrées, [67] ont émergé de l'analyse.

Dans le cadre de ce chapitre, seuls les arguments liés aux freins con- 108
cernant le management de la justice ont été exploités. Plus précisément, les nœuds[68] traitant directement («réticence au management») ou indirectement (notamment: «juges individualistes» ou encore «juge n'a pas de compte à rendre») de cette question ont été exploités. Etant donné la richesse de la matière récoltée (près de 1000 pages de retranscription), une exploitation intégrale des entretiens ne paraissait pas pertinente. Cela peut être considéré comme une limite à la présente méthode, de même que le choix de l'échantillon des personnes interviewées, qui n'a pas été consti-

---

ment. Les cantons alémaniques de Lucerne et Schaffhouse ont été considérés à des fins de comparaison.

65 STRAUSS/CORBIN (2004).

66 Ceci signifie que les entretiens ont été arrêtés lorsqu'aucun nouvel argument ne venait enrichir les récits précédents. Voir MARTINEAU (2005).

67 ROBERT/BOUILLAGUET (2002).

68 Les nœuds sont des regroupements de citations sur le même thème, définis empiriquement par les chercheurs.

tué selon une méthode représentative. Toutefois, il est utile de rappeler que le principe de *saturation qualitative* retenu a de bonnes chances de refléter une partie significative de la réalité du pouvoir judiciaire actuel en Suisse.

4. Résultats

109 Les discours tenus par les différentes parties prenantes de la justice recèlent de très nombreux arguments susceptibles d'expliquer pourquoi il est difficile d'introduire des logiques et instruments de management dans les organisations du pouvoir judiciaire. Ces arguments sont mis tout particulièrement en exergue par les juges eux-mêmes, mais ils ne sont de loin pas les seuls à le faire. Rappelons en outre que les arguments présentés ci-dessous ne sont pas la réponse à une question spécifique qui aurait été axée sur «les freins à l'introduction du management au sein du pouvoir judiciaire», mais ressortent bien en filigrane des réponses spontanément fournies à l'ensemble des questions du guide d'entretien.

Milieu de la justice en général (l'institution)

110 Le milieu de la justice est tout d'abord qualifié de «conservateur», peu ouvert au changement, voire résistant au changement amené par le management: «la justice est incapable de se remettre en question [...] c'est le droit, rien que le droit, mais on oublie le justiciable, on oublie la réputation qu'ils (les juges) se font...». Cette résistance, présente peu ou prou dans tout type d'organisation, se nourrit au sein de la justice d'une méfiance *a priori* face à des méthodes peu adaptées au pouvoir judiciaire. Ainsi, certains interlocuteurs relèvent une forme de blocage culturel fondamental: «L'ouverture au management va évoluer lentement, il y a une vraie allergie à ça». La justice apparaît posée sur un piédestal qui la place au-dessus d'autres logiques d'action, notamment celles mises en avant par le management. L'institution judiciaire aime en outre à soigner une forme de culture du secret: un juge qui assumait pourtant des responsabilités managériales nous a par exemple confié que «Les communications au niveau de la justice sont toujours un peu délicates car certaines choses doivent rester secrètes alors que d'autres choses doivent vraiment être communiquées». Ce constat peut s'avérer problématique dans la mesure où le manque de transparence sur son fonctionnement peut conduire à une réelle opacité pour les autres parties prenantes, le management étant – implicitement ou explicitement- vu comme ouvrant une brèche dans cette

culture. Différents arguments liés aux juges en général (cf ci-dessous) viendront renforcer ces éléments.

Justice en tant qu'organisation publique (l'institution)

La justice est volontiers assimilée par certains de nos interlocuteurs à une organisation publique, organisation à laquelle différents travers sont associés et qui est peu favorable à l'introduction d'une logique managériale: «cela reste une administration». L'administration étant formée de fonctionnaires «à qui on ne peut pas imposer quelque chose», et qui «se comportent comme des fonctionnaires» sont des points qui mettent en lumière que le registre *bureaucratique* est allègrement intégré dans l'univers symbolique auquel la justice est assimilée. En même temps, il est relevé que ce que l'administration peut faire, la justice devrait également en être capable: «Oft heisst es, ihr könnt ruhig etwas sparen, weil die Verwaltung das auch kann».[69] Cette affirmation est d'autant plus intéressante que le pouvoir judiciaire met a contrario un point d'honneur, selon plusieurs de nos interlocuteurs, à ne pas être assimilée à l'administration publique, à être différente et ainsi, à ne pas être traitée (notamment par les autorités politiques) de la même manière que l'administration.[70] 111

Les autorités politiques (in-dépendance de la Justice)

L'indépendance de la justice, tout particulièrement vis-à-vis du pouvoir politique, contribue à la résistance au mouvement de managérialisation de la justice, dans la mesure où celui-ci est vu comme un moyen de renforcer le contrôle du politique sur la justice, de rendre plus transparent son fonctionnement et ses «résultats». La spécificité helvétique liée à l'élection (et en l'occurrence à la *réélection*) des juges par le Parlement renforce l'argument précédent, en ce sens que les statistiques et autres indicateurs liés au travail des juges sont susceptibles de peser négativement sur ces derniers lors de leur réélection, ce qui pourrait être assimilé à une brèche dans l'indépendance du pouvoir judiciaire. 112

---

69 « Souvent on nous dit que vous [la justice] vous pouvez aussi économiser, puisque l'administration le peut ».

70 Ce qui n'est pas évident lorsque l'on analyse la « dépendance administrative » du pouvoir judiciaire dans de nombreux cantons, une dépendance qui apparaît notamment dans le processus budgétaire, informatique et ressources humaines, voire les bâtiments…

Milieu des juges en général (liés aux acteurs-clés, professionnels de la justice)

113 Au cœur de l'appareil judiciaire se trouvent les juges, des personnes et personnalités affublées de nombreux qualificatifs généraux a priori peu favorables aux logiques de management. Relevons en particulier des personnalités fortes, indépendantes, résistantes au changement et se plaisant dans leurs habitudes, voire leurs routines («on a toujours fait comme ça»), des personnalités parfois nostalgiques d'une époque où «on avait le temps».[71] Les juges n'acceptent des consignes ou contrôles de personne, ou alors uniquement de leurs pairs et encore, mais en tous les cas pas de «non juristes» managers: «Richter sind halt Häuptlige und mit mehreren Häuptligen wird's immer schwieriger»[72]. Il s'agit d'un argument à mettre en parallèle avec le fait que, dans une telle culture, «les pairs n'osent rien dire aux collègues», ou encore: «ça serait étrange de demander à nos collègues de nous rendre des comptes, de tenir un décompte de leurs vacances, ce n'est pas tellement dans l'esprit». Ce qui revient au final à dire que «le juge n'a à recevoir d'ordre de personne». Certaines des personnes rencontrées soulignent encore que de par son métier, «le juge aime avoir raison», et que certains d'entre eux «sont déconnectés des réalités du terrain». Des réalités, telles que le temps réellement à disposition ou les moyens matériels disponibles, que le management va contribuer à révéler.

Métier/profession de juge (liés aux acteurs-clés de la justice)

114 Les juges ont suivi un parcours formationnel spécifique et sont élus (ou nommés) pour «dire le droit, et pas s'occuper d'administratif». Cet argument est parfois accentué par l'idée que la fonction de juge correspond à une forme de vocation qui exprime des motivations profondes qui ne devraient pas être détournées sur des activités relevant du management. D'ailleurs, les juges «ne s'intéressent pas au management», et ne souhaitent pas se charger de ce type de responsabilité: «als Richter muss man das nicht noch im Rücksack haben».[73] Car ces responsabilités pourraient les empêcher de faire leur travail de base: «non seulement on ne peut plus

---

[71] La dimension générationnelle de cet argument n'échappera pas au lecteur, et a été fréquemment mise en avant par nos interlocuteurs, sans toutefois faire l'unanimité, certaines personnes relevant «qu'il s'agit avant tout d'une question de personnalité, et non d'âge…!».

[72] Les juges sont des personnages, chefs (de tribu), et avec plusieurs chefs, c'est délicat.

[73] En tant que juge, on ne doit pas encore mettre cela dans son sac à dos.

faire son travail normalement, mais en plus on fait mal son travail de procureur général». Leur confier des responsabilités pourrait conduire à diminuer l'intérêt pour leur fonction, tout en produisant des sortes de juges hybrides qui ne seraient ni bons en tant que juges ni en tant que managers. Il s'agirait alors d'une voie à éviter car les juges ne sont pas formés au management, ne seraient pas aptes à diriger du personnel ni prêts à suivre de la formation pour cela («Weiterbildung macht man nicht»).[74] Si tant est que cela soit utile, car être un bon administrateur semble inné pour nos interlocuteurs. A contrario, les juges doivent absolument diriger le pouvoir judiciaire: «Comme c'est l'expression de la volonté du troisième pouvoir, il doit être défendu, vécu par un magistrat sinon il y aurait une différence de niveau d'interlocuteur quand on s'adresse au Conseil d'Etat». Ceci montre bien que la fonction de gestionnaire est considérée par les juges comme subordonnée à ces derniers.

Inadéquation des concepts et outils du management (arguments plus spécifiquement liés au management)

Beaucoup d'arguments peuvent être cités sur ce thème. A commencer 115
par le fait que le management et l'administration sont un art mineur («eine niedriegere Kunst») par rapport au droit, et qu'il s'agit d'un phénomène de mode, sous-entendu amené à disparaître. Toujours dans le préambule, le management est inapproprié à l'institution judiciaire («qui n'est pas une fabrique de chaussettes»), son adoption conduirait à assimiler de manière simplifiée les tribunaux à des entreprises de production industrielle, ce qui n'est absolument pas comparable. Dans le même registre, le vocabulaire du management ne convient pas au pouvoir judiciaire: des mots tels que productivité, clients, produits, ne correspondent guère à la spécificité de l'activité des tribunaux. De manière plus spécifique, le management serait inapproprié parce que ces notions/concepts principaux ne s'appliquent guère à l'action du pouvoir judiciaire:

Les objectifs: le pouvoir judiciaire ne travaille pas par objectifs, il doit 116
traiter les cas qui lui sont soumis, en respect du droit.

Les indicateurs: ne sont pas pertinents car la «mesure» de l'activité est 117
trompeuse, est uniquement quantitative alors que la qualité est essentielle dans le travail du tribunal/du juge, et «qu'on peut faire dire n'importe quoi à des indicateurs». En sus, la saisie et la gestion des indicateurs nécessitent des ressources disproportionnées par rapport à leur utilité réelle.

[74] On ne fait pas de formation continue, cela ne se fait pas.

118 Les clients: concept particulièrement inapproprié à la justice, ce terme met en exergue le choix et le niveau de qualité souhaité par le client, au contraire du *justiciable* qui, dans la logique démocratique et constitutionnelle, bénéficie du même niveau de prestation que tout autre citoyen ayant affaire avec la justice. Au demeurant, la justice et les parties ne sont pas sur le même niveau: «[…] die «Kunden» sind keine freiwilligen Vertargspartner, die auf gleicher Augenhöhe mit der Justiz stehen».[75] De surcroit, il est relevé que «le management ne sert pas les clients», ne contribue donc pas à la qualité des jugements prononcés.

119 Les produits: on retrouve ici le même type d'argument: «on n'a pas un produit qu'on va vendre, on chercherait même à diminuer notre clientèle idéalement…».

120 La reddition de compte/l'imputabilité: le travail du juge doit être conforme au droit, mais il ne doit pas rendre des comptes, à personne, même pas aux collègues: «quand on est juge et qu'on a rendu son verdict, on est en paix avec soi-même, on n'a plus de justification à faire». A cet égard, il est encore relevé que le tribunal/le juge n'ont guère de *feedback* sur leur activité (hormis par le biais des recours éventuels).

121 Le budget: pratique qui s'applique difficilement, car «on doit traiter ce qui vient», l'utilité d'une *enveloppe budgétaire* n'est ainsi pas comprise.

122 Le chef/la hiérarchie: le juge n'a pas de chef qui le dirigerait véritablement, et s'il existe (Président de cour par exemple), celui-ci n'a pas d'ordre à donner, ni ne contrôle l'activité exercée, comme l'illustre cette citation: «comment vous permettez-vous de vous mêler des affaires de ma secrétaire, c'est mon affaire». L'autonomie et l'indépendance des juges (cf ci-dessus), l'individualisme de leurs méthodes de travail, et leur caractère généralement fort, sont autant d'éléments défavorables à la position de chef: «dans la justice, on a affaire à des rois qui ont de la peine à lâcher du lest à quelqu'un». De plus, l'introduction de techniques managériales pourrait casser la logique de la confiance, pour la remplacer par celle des ordres et du contrôle d'exécution. Or comme l'affirme une personne interviewée: «tant que ça va, pas besoin d'intervenir». A noter que ce point fait l'objet d'un développement approfondi dans le dernier chapitre de cet ouvrage.

---

[75] Les « clients » ne sont pas des co-contractants libres, se situant au même niveau que la justice.

L'équipe: elle bien présente dans les pratiques de management actuelles, mais la notion d'équipe se heurte au légendaire individualisme des juges. 123

La valorisation (*incentives*): c'est une pratique inexistante, et qui serait inappropriée au fonctionnement de la justice. 124

Les managers en tant que fonction exercée (arguments plus spécifiquement liés au management, qu'il soit exercé par des juges, ou non, cette dernière option étant naturellement la plus critiquée)

Il est relevé que les managers, là où ils ont été introduits, «ne connaissent ou ne comprennent pas l'activité des juges». Ils contribuent à une forme de technocratisation qui aurait tendance à dépersonnaliser ou déshumaniser l'activité du tribunal, et peuvent amener une forme de déresponsabilisation des juges quant au fonctionnement de leur activité (puisque cela relèverait alors du manager en place, comme l'illustre cette citation: «le secrétaire général se charge des problèmes dont les juges ne veulent pas s'occuper»). Ainsi, les managers doivent faire face à une méfiance fondamentale de la part des juges, surtout si ces derniers ne sont pas intégrés dans les décisions qu'ils prennent, alors que si les managers sont considérés comme une *fonction* exercée par des juges, ces derniers vont mal exercer autant l'un que l'autre de ces deux rôles (juges et managers, cf ci-dessus). 125

Caractéristiques d'une «bonne justice» (liés au processus juridique lui-même)

Les freins à l'introduction d'une logique managériale sont également à rechercher du côté de la conception d'une «bonne justice». Tout d'abord et en bonne place, la rapidité, mise au centre des actions de management, pourrait nuire à la qualité des jugements, à l'exhaustivité de la prise en compte des arguments mis en avant par les parties, aboutissant à une forme de déshumanisation de la justice pas propice à «l'orientation-client» mise en avant par les managers eux-mêmes. «On prend le temps qu'il faut» pour traiter les cas soumis, ce qui indique un rapport au temps particulier qui évite de négliger les cas, comme le montre cette citation: «A mon avis, ça ne va pas dans le bon sens, une justice rapide c'est bien, mais on doit pouvoir prendre le temps de traiter une affaire». Ou encore cette autre citation qui puise dans le registre musical: «Eine Klaviersonate von Beethoven kann man schon ein bisschen schneller spielen. Aber wenn 126 man zu schnell spielt, dann ist es kein Beethoven mehr. So ähnlich ist es mit unserer Arbeit“.[76] Plutôt que de mettre la pression sur la gestion du temps, il s'agirait au contraire que le management puisse renforcer le processus judiciaire en tant que tel: «moi, je prends le temps qu'il faudra pour traiter une affaire, et je me fous que d'autres [affaires] s'accumulent, ce n'est pas ma faute, c'est parce qu'on n'est pas assez nombreux». Le travail du juge nécessite calme et sérénité, alors que le management introduit du stress et peut conduire à une ambiance tendue.

Nouveau code de procédure (liés au processus juridique lui-même)

127 L'introduction de ce nouveau code a complexifié et ralenti la procédure dans son ensemble, ce qui fait dire à plusieurs de nos interlocuteurs qu'il n'est guère compatible avec l'introduction d'une logique managériale (dont la finalité supposée consiste justement à réduire le temps de traitement des procédures).

Modalités d'organisation actuelles (liées au fonctionnement en place dans les Tribunaux)

128 Certaines modalités organisationnelles ne favorisent pas une managérialisation des tribunaux. Relevons notamment le fait que sur certains dossiers, le regard de plusieurs juges est requis (typiquement trois juges avant d'arrêter le jugement), ce qui ralentit immanquablement le processus, ou encore le fait que dans certains cantons, l'activité du procureur général échappe à la haute surveillance de la justice, ce qui fait «qu'il fait ce qu'il veut…».

Conduite du changement/des réformes dans la justice (liés au fonctionnement actuel)

129 Finalement, certains freins à l'introduction du management sont à mettre en lien avec la conduite des projets d'organisation/de gestion introduits ces dernières années. Ces différentes citations l'illustrent: «les actions de management introduites ces dernières années n'apportent rien», «ce sont des actions alibi», il y en a trop à la fois et elles ont tendance à s'annuler. Ou encore la précision suivante: il faut d'abord «que le management fasse ses preuves» pour apprécier son réel potentiel à améliorer le fonctionnement des tribunaux. Finalement, un appel au politique: «Das

[76] Une sonate de Beethoven peut être jouée avec un tempo un peu plus rapide. Mais si on la joue trop vite, alors ce n'est plus du Beethoven. C'est un peu la même chose avec notre travail.

Parlament sollte öfters sagen, das lassen wir jetzt sein, das bringt euch nichts, dann haben wir mehr Zeit fürs Kerngeschäft“.[77]

5. Discussion

5.1 Valeurs institutionnelles et management

Troisième pouvoir indépendant par la conception même du système démocratique, la justice n'en est pas moins dépendante du politique du point de vue des ressources attribuées et de la haute surveillance politique exercée.[78] Cette position ambiguë de l'institution judiciaire met quelque peu à mal le piédestal sur lequel elle aime à se situer, en-dessus voire en-dehors des autres institutions et de la société, de laquelle elle doit se distancer pour dire le droit en complète indépendance, sans rendre des comptes à d'autres, qu'à la vérité. L'univers symbolique de la justice semble ainsi marqué par une conception de supériorité, d'éloignement et de secret, fort peu propice à l'introduction d'une logique managériale. En effet, les techniques de management visent la maîtrise, la transparence et l'imputabilité des institutions pilotées[79], dans le but d'en influencer la destinée. Dans cette optique, la crainte de voir le contrôle politique renforcé, et par conséquent l'indépendance de la justice mise à mal, paraît légitime: «si les juges doivent expliquer au management pourquoi un cas a pris plus de temps que la norme, chaque fois que cela arrive, alors l'indépendante de la justice est compromise» .[80] Dans ce contexte, la seule voie possible serait alors une forme d'auto-management, qui a contrario pourrait renforcer l'indépendance de la justice. Selon Vigour,[81] cette forme d'auto-management serait une voie intéressante pour restaurer la confiance des citoyens dans la justice. Dans le cadre de la Belgique dont elle retrace les réformes, elle serait appuyée par certains magistrats soucieux de rétablir la légitimité de l'institution. Une tendance relevée dans d'autres rapports évaluant les réformes de la justice, où l'efficacité et 130

77 Le parlement devrait dire plus souvent qu'il laisse tomber ceci [des projets de réformes, de management], que ça nous apporte rien, comme ça on aurait plus de temps pour le cœur de notre activité.

78 MAHON/SCHALLER (2013).

79 BARTOLI (2005).

80 EMERY /DE SANTIS (2013), p. 16.

81 VIGOUR (2008).

l'efficience sont des variables importantes pour améliorer la confiance de la population dans la justice.[82]

131 Selon un avocat interrogé, «c'est plus difficile de faire changer la justice, car il y a cette sacro-sainte culture de l'indépendance, interprétée à toutes les modes et toutes les sauces, à partir du moment où on fait partie de l'ordre judiciaire, on est intouchable, incontrôlable». Une affirmation intéressante par rapport à un autre argument évoqué par nos interlocuteurs: la tentative d'assimiler l'institution judiciaire à un ensemble plus grand auquel appartient également l'administration: le secteur (ou service) public. Un détour intéressant, puisque l'administration publique a intégré très largement les nouvelles méthodes de management, en recherche à la fois d'une efficacité et d'une efficience accrues, mais également d'une nouvelle légitimité face aux critiques endurantes de la population et des élus[83]. Une administration de plus en plus soumise aux exigences de transparence (cf loi sur la transparence)[84] et de performance (selon la nouvelle loi sur l'organisation du gouvernement et de l'administration, LOGA).[85] Mais un détour qui apporte alors également la face moins reluisante de l'administration publique: son univers de référence bureaucratique, affublé de multiples qualificatifs reflétant les tares intemporelles de l'appareil public, ainsi que des fonctionnaires qui le peuplent: lenteur, inefficience, fonctionnement poussiéreux, figé et redondant, pour ne citer que les principaux stéréotypes véhiculés par l'imaginaire administratif, souvent éloigné de la réalité.[86] Il n'empêche que ce côté négatif de l'administration, à laquelle la justice est assimilée, renforce la pression à la managérialisation de la justice, en particulier par les responsables politiques pris dans le mécanisme délicat de la haute surveillance de la justice.[87] Dans le même registre, relevons le fait que l'institution judiciaire serait empreinte d'un conservatisme la rendant résistante à tout changement exogène, un défaut qui est également typique de l'administration, forme institutionnelle parmi les plus résistantes au changement décrété de l'extérieur.[88]

---

82 Emery /De Santis (2013).
83 Emery (2011).
84 LTrans, RS 152.3 selon la législation suisse.
85 RS 172.010.
86 Du Gay (2005).
87 Poltier (2012).
88 Crozier (1980).

Finalement, les qualités attribuées à une bonne justice, notamment l'analyse minutieuse et exhaustive des éléments litigieux, la justice procédurale et distributive au fondement de son activité ainsi que l'humanité nécessaire à un jugement respectueux des parties, sont perçues comme antinomiques aux exigences de productivité, voire de rentabilité, véhiculées par le management. On mesure ici à quel point l'univers de référence de la justice, monde civique par excellence au sens de Boltanski et Thévenot,[89] ne se marie pas à celui du monde industriel, issu du taylorisme et de la recherche effrénée de productivité qui l'accompagne. Nous avons d'ailleurs remarqué dans une étude similaire que les juges font très peu appel à la logique «industrielle» par rapport à d'autres employés du secteur public suisse.[90] 132

La difficulté réside pourtant dans le fait qu'une justice lente n'est pas une justice de qualité, voire représente un déni de justice: c'est dire que l'on fait face à une valeur qui, néanmoins, est partie intégrante de l'univers du pouvoir judiciaire, puisque des voies de recours sont prévues tant dans les codes de procédure civile que pénale. Nous sommes ici en présence de valeurs hybrides, susceptibles de favoriser le mariage entre les cultures judiciaire et managériale, à l'image des valeurs portées par l'univers en émergence de la post-bureaucratie.[91] 133

5.2 Culture des tribunaux et management

«Or, voici que l'économie, par son avatar managérial, prétend non plus infléchir le droit, mais le supplanter. Le management est une alternative à la procédure».[92] Cette citation constitue une excellente introduction à l'univers organisationnel des Tribunaux, que nos interlocuteurs estiment fort peu adapté à l'exploitation concrète des outils de management. Et cela commence par le vocabulaire utilisé, inspiré d'un univers mercantile ou consumériste[93] auquel l'activité judiciaire ne correspond guère: le justiciable a droit à un procès équitable, mené par un juge neutre et indépendant, mais sans toutefois pouvoir le choisir; le consommateur, lui, achète un produit à la mesure de ses besoins, selon ses préférences et 134

89 BOLTANSKI/THÉVENOT (1991).
90 EMERY/DE SANTIS (2014).
91 EMERY/DE SANTIS (2013).
92 MARTENS (2013), P. 108.
93 VIGOUR (2008).

choix personnels. Mais en la matière également, l'ambiguïté issue d'une valeur hybride doit être relevée: *l'orientation-client*, typique de la nouvelle gestion publique, trouve également un nombre croissant de supporters au sein des Tribunaux, non pas tant dans le vocabulaire lui-même, largement rejeté, mais dans les comportements et actions concrètes que cette orientation suppose. Il s'agit notamment d'être à l'écoute du justiciable, de lui faciliter ses démarches, de s'exprimer dans un langage compréhensible et d'évaluer, indépendamment du fait qu'il a ou non eu gain de cause, son niveau de satisfaction (voir les enquêtes qui se multiplient, également en Suisse, pouvoir judiciaire genevois, bernois, par exemple).

135 Cette résistance à la managérialisation continue avec moult exemples illustrant les irréductibles différences entre une entreprise industrielle et la justice. Notons tout d'abord que la comparaison est faite avec des fabriques, pour souligner le caractère industriel, et non avec des entreprises de services, auxquelles la justice pourrait être plus aisément comparée. Or il s'agit là de deux mondes, largement analysés quant à leurs différences essentielles:[94] produire un service suppose un processus interactionnel qui est bien présent dans la justice, notamment lors des auditions, durant lesquelles le juge peut donner au justiciable le sentiment d'être entendu et pris au sérieux.

136 L'inadéquation des outils de management touche le répertoire complet à disposition, nos interlocuteurs invoquant une logique fonctionnelle unique du tribunal: absence de produit, de client, d'objectifs, d'indicateurs de performance et de besoin de rendre des comptes. Rendre la justice serait avant tout un processus soumis à des exigences professionnelles, dont le flux d'entrée n'est guère planifiable, plutôt que la livraison de prestations correspondant à des objectifs fixés par une direction.

137 Autre difficulté: la figure du manager-chef, autorité hiérarchique investi d'une forme de leadership sur les juges. Que cette fonction soit assumée par un juriste ou non ne change pas fondamentalement la critique. En effet, s'il s'agit d'un pair, alors celui-ci doit respecter ses collègues «qui n'attendent d'ordre de personne, pas même d'un collègue»; alors que s'il s'agit d'un non-juriste, la légitimité et la compétence même de la personne sont d'emblée remises en question, notamment par le fait que la justice devrait être dirigée par un magistrat, de manière à pouvoir se situer au même rang que le pouvoir politique (membre de l'exécutif) et représenter

---

[94] NORMANN (1994).

crédiblement les intérêts du pouvoir judiciaire. Au surplus, la fonction de manager est susceptible de déresponsabiliser les juges (des quelques responsabilités de management qui leur incombent, par exemple des membres de leur équipe, greffiers et secrétaires), tout en technocratisant le fonctionnement du tribunal, qui n'en a guère besoin.

L'univers managérial est ainsi assimilé à un regain technocratique, ar- 138
gument qui s'inscrit dans la critique du courant classique du management,[95] duquel entendent justement se démarquer les approches contemporaines du management public,[96] même si les expériences concrètes ont montré que cela n'était de loin pas évident.[97] Les inconvénients supposément issus des méthodes de management touchent également la dimension humaine du fonctionnement du tribunal: elles sont susceptibles de miner le climat de confiance et de collaboration, générer un stress inutile et, au final, ne servent guère le justiciable. Les acteurs de la justice reprennent ici la critique s'adressant plus généralement au management, véhiculant une culture du contrôle et de la récompense/sanction peu propice à des relations de coopération fructueuses, si ce n'est plus radicalement, pour introduire de nouvelles formes de domination dans l'organisation du tribunal.[98]

Dans le même registre, les expériences de management des tribunaux 139
en cours n'auraient apporté aucun résultat et relèveraient de l'alibi politique, les juges continuant à travailler selon leurs habitudes, ce qui nous amène au dernier niveau d'analyse: la dimension professionnelle de la culture judiciaire.

5.3 Culture professionnelle des juges et management

De nombreux arguments avancés relèvent, peu ou prou, de la 140
dimension professionnelle de la culture des juges. A commencer par la très typique revendication à l'*autonomie*, par opposition à l'*hétéronomie*, qui implique que seuls les professionnels peuvent, entre eux, définir les exigences de qualité du travail réalisé. Constat qui place toute activité de management exercée par une personne non juriste en situation délicate pour ne pas dire illégitime, ce d'autant qu'à cette auto-référence profes-

95 BOYER/EQUILBEY (1990).
96 HABLÜTZEL/HALDEMANN/SCHEDLER/SCHWAAR (1995).
97 NORMAN (2007), HUFTY (1998).
98 GIAUQUE (2006).

sionnelle vient s'ajouter la légitimité conférée par la fonction de *magistrat élu*. Ce dernier point est intéressant puisque la dimension politique sous-jacente au processus d'élection constitue un point de résistance supplémentaire par rapport au caractère potentiellement intrusif des outils de management, particulièrement ceux destinés à évaluer la qualité du travail fourni par les juges.[99] Quant aux interventions de management exercées par les pairs, celles-ci sont alors soumises à une double contrainte au sens de Watzlawick, Weakland et al,[100] c'est-à-dire que les injonctions relevant du management ne peuvent venir que des pairs, mais en même temps, les pairs doivent respecter leurs collègues, notamment l'autonomie, valeur constituante de l'identité professionnelle des juges, et ainsi ne pas intervenir dans leur sphère d'activité. Bien dire le droit, comme l'exprime l'un des juges interrogés, c'est être en paix avec soi-même, soulignant, s'il en était encore besoin, l'importance de *l'auto-nomie*.

141 Un autre élément au centre de l'activité professionnelle des juges est le fait «d'avoir raison» de par la logique même du processus judiciaire, autre obstacle aux interventions du management, même si ces dernières ne portent pas sur l'activité de juger en tant que telle, mais sur des éléments périphériques tels que l'organisation et les méthodes de travail des juges. Un point d'ailleurs souvent renforcé par le fait que les juges montrent fréquemment une forte personnalité, rendant l'activité de management plus délicate.

142 L'ethos professionnel des juges comprend également l'idée de détachement de la situation jugée, afin de garder la hauteur nécessaire à un jugement équitable.[101] Ce qui fait dire à certains de nos interlocuteurs que les juges sont volontiers déconnectés des réalités «matérielles» du processus de production judiciaire, traitées avant tout par les interventions de management. Déconnexion intéressante révélant une forme d'immatérialité de l'acte judiciaire, idéalement affranchi des contraintes liées aux ressources disponibles. Ainsi, lorsqu'un juge affirme «moi, je prends le temps qu'il faudra pour traiter une affaire, et je me fous que d'autres [affaires] s'accumulent», cela traduit ce détachement vers l'immatérialité du temps, ainsi que la volonté de ne pas assumer les conséquences d'un tel

[99] MAHON/SCHALLER (2013).
[100] WATZLAWICK/WEAKLAND/FISCH (1975).
[101] LUDEWIG (2008), LUDEWIG/WEISLEHNER/ANGEHRN (2007).

comportement sur la gestion des ressources disponibles pour l'ensemble des activités à réaliser au sein d'un tribunal.

Les juges sont comparés par certains de nos interlocuteurs à des rois (une figure utilisée, soit-dit-en passant, aussi pour les managers), ce qui les positionne clairement en-dessus des autres (professions ou fonctions), et l'art qu'ils pratiquent est présenté comme majeur, contrairement au management décrit comme art mineur (cf citation mise en épigraphe introductif). L'on y perçoit ici non seulement une échelle de valeur décrivant une hiérarchie entre les professions, certaines plus prestigieuses que d'autres, mais également la fonction de support que les activités managériales pourraient apporter aux processus centraux de la justice. Ce qui dénote d'une confusion entre processus de soutien (gérant les ressources telles que les finances, les RH ou encore l'informatique), et les processus de management,[102] lesquels ont pour mission de piloter l'institution vers une vision, élaborée par les parties prenantes et permettant de concrétiser sa mission. 143

Suit un ensemble d'arguments relevant davantage de la motivation, des intérêts, voire de la vocation des juges, formés au droit pour l'exercer, et non pour consacrer du temps à des activités administratives. Ce point, que l'on retrouve dans tout type de profession fortement affirmée (voir le débat autour des assistants administratifs dans les domaines de la police, de l'éducation, du social, etc.),[103] illustre encore une fois le primat du cœur du métier sur des activités annexes ou de support, qui devraient être déléguées à d'autres fonctions que celle des juges. Mais qui place ces derniers devant un autre dilemme: celui de lâcher une partie de leur pouvoir, puisque toute activité administrative interagit, même minimalement, avec l'activité principale qui la génère. Dans ce contexte, un juge exerçant sa fonction principale *et* celle de gestionnaire, voire de manager du tribunal, risque fortement «de faire mal les deux», de se retrouver en qualité d'*hybride*, n'assumant ni pleinement sa fonction de juge, ni celle de manager. Or le caractère hybride recèle toujours à la fois un potentiel à développer,[104] mais également un risque de confusion des genres. Un risque qui ne manquera pas de se réaliser à partir du moment où les juges ne montrent par une propension particulièrement développée à la formation 144

[102] GILLET-GOINARD/SENO (2011).
[103] KESSLER/BACH/HERON (2007).
[104] EMERY/GIAUQUE, 2014.

continue, hormis dans le registre de l'actualisation des connaissances juridiques.[105]

6. Conclusion

145 Au final, la dimension culturelle met en lumière de nombreux obstacles à la managérialisation de la justice. Si la culture professionnelle des juges et l'ethos sous-jacent qui les animent dans leurs comportements au quotidien semblent cristalliser les obstacles, il ne faudrait pas sous-estimer la dimension organisationnelle de la culture. Nombreux sont les auteurs à souligner le caractère réducteur de la métaphore «industrielle» du tribunal, laquelle fait ressortir à quel point l'*organisation* tribunal, au sens de la théorie des organisations,[106] n'est pas pensée comme un processus de production, supporté par des ressources pour atteindre des objectifs stratégiques. Au-delà du vocabulaire qui, déjà, repousse le monde judiciaire, on mesure à quel point l'univers de représentation managériale apparaît aujourd'hui encore assez éloigné de l'univers du tribunal. Quant à la dimension institutionnelle de la culture du pouvoir judiciaire, c'est sans doute la couche la plus profonde de la variable culturelle qui est ici interpelée. Le rôle symbolique développé par l'appareil judiciaire dans la société, ses sources de légitimité traditionnelles, ancrées dans la Constitution ainsi que dans l'histoire de cette institution, sont autant de caractéristiques consubstantielles à la justice, qui pourraient bien constituer l'obstacle le plus résistant à sa managérialisation.

146 De par la méthode suivie, cette étude présente différentes limites qu'il convient de rappeler.

147 Ainsi, le fait que les thèmes inventoriés dans les «nœuds» codifiés par l'équipe de recherche rassemblent l'ensemble des arguments mentionnés par nos différents interlocuteurs, quelles que soient les fonctions assumées par ces derniers, pousse naturellement à une amplification des freins mis en exergue dans le présent chapitre. En particulier, il eut été intéressant de différencier la perception des freins potentiels à la managérialisation entre les juges eux-mêmes et les autres acteurs de la justice, qu'ils soient internes au pouvoir judiciaire (greffiers, personnel administratifs), mais aussi externes (responsables politiques, journalistes, auxiliaires de la jus-

105 LANGBROEK/MAHONEY (2008).
106 MINTZBERG (1982).

tice notamment), une analyse prévue dans la prochaine phase de la recherche. Ensuite, le traitement de l'ensemble des arguments mentionnés par nos interlocuteurs, sous l'angle des freins à la managérialisation, peut à tort faire penser que ceux-ci sont tous présents en même temps au sein des tribunaux suisses, ce qui n'est évidemment pas le cas. Et dans le même registre, les éléments susceptibles de constituer des leviers favorables à la managérialisation ne sont pas traités dans cet article.

D'autre part, la saturation des arguments obtenues grâce à ce pro- 148
gramme d'entretiens n'implique toutefois pas que les arguments mentionnés soient représentatifs de la population étudiée (les tribunaux suisses) ni ne puissent être extrapolés à l'ensemble de ces tribunaux, puisque seuls deux cantons suisses alémaniques et le Tessin ont été retenus en plus des cantons romands (sauf Genève). Mais la méthode retenue ne visait pas une telle généralisation.

Si les scénarios extrêmes mentionnés en ce qui concerne les relations 149
entre profession et management (rejet du management, ou domination complète du management) sont manifestement à rejeter, les deux variantes intermédiaires relevées par Ferlie et Geraghty se distinguent plus subtilement, et pourraient bien marquer la nuance ténue entre un management au service de l'activité judiciaire, scénario soutenu par une partie des juges rencontrés, et une activité judiciaire au service d'un management devenu fin en lui-même, nouvelle légitimité d'un appareil bureaucratique en qui le public a perdu confiance, comme cela a été mis en exergue pour l'administration publique plus généralement.[107] Seul l'avenir montrera la voie préférentiellement suivie.

7. Bibliographie citée

Alt, E. (2013). La justice au défi du nouveau management. Quel management pour quelle justice? T. D. Marchandise. Bruxelles, Larcier: 89-105.

Amadieu, J.-F. (2012). DRH. Le livre noir. Paris, Seuil.

Bartoli, A. (2005). Le management dans les organisations publiques. Paris, Dunod.

[107] EMERY/GIAUQUE (2005).

Bernard, B., A. Drumaux, et al. (2012). La justice pénale en prospective - Six scénarios à l'horizon 2020. Bruxelles, Belgium, Bruylant.

Bezes, P. (2003). Du management public au new public management: fabrique, diffusion et appropriation des idées néo-managériales dans les réformes administratives en France. Une génération de réformes en management public: et après?, Strasbourg, Politiques et management public.

Bloor, G. and P. Dawson (1994). "Understanding Professional Culture in Organizational Context." Organization Studies 15(2): 275-295.

Boltanski, L. and L. Thévenot (1991). De la justification. Les économies de la grandeur. Paris, Gallimard.

Bouckaert, G. (2007). Cultural Characteristics From Public Management Reforms Worldwide. Cultural Aspects of Public Management Reform. K. Schedler and I. Proeller. UK, Elsevier. 16: 29-64.

Boyer, L. and N. Equilbey (1990). Histoire du management. Paris, Les Editions d'organisation.

Buschor, E. and K. Schedler (1995). Perspectives on performance measurement and Public Secteur accounting. Berne, Haupt.

Carboni, N. (2008). Professional Autonomy vs. Political Control: how to deal with the dilemma. Some evidence from the Italian core executive. EGPA annual Conference 2008, Innovation in the public sector. Rotterdam.

Church, T. W. (1985). "Examining Local Legal Culture." American Bar Foundation Research Journal 10(3): 449-518.

Collerette, P. and R. Schneider (2004). Le pilotage du changement, une approche stratégique et pratique. Montréal, Les presses de l'Université du Québec.

Commission européenne pour l'efficacité de la justice (2010). Manuel pour la réalisation d'enquêtes de satisfaction auprès des usagers des tribunaux des Etat membres du Conseil de l'Europe. Les études de la CEPEJ. Strasbourg, Conseil de l'Europe. 15: 1-35.

Coolsen, J. P. (2008). "Case Management Innovation in a Large, Urban Trial Court: The Critical Importance of Legal Stakeholder Attitudes." The Justice System Journal 30(1): 70-90.

Crozier, M. (1980). La société bloquée. Paris, Point-politique.

de Gaulejac, V. and A. Mercier (2012). Manifeste pour sortir du mal-être au travail. Bruxelles, Desclée de Brouwer.

Deal, T. E. and A. A. Kennedy (1982). Corporate cultures: the rites and rituals of corporate life, Addison-Wesley Publishing Compagny.

Delley, J.-D. (1994). Quand l'esprit d'entreprise vient à l'Etat: pour une réforme du service public. Lausanne, Domaine public.

Denhardt, J.-V. and R. B. Denhardt (2003). The New Public Service: Serving, Not Steering. Armonk, NY, M.E.Sharpe.

Desmarais, C., G. Jeannot, et al. (2007). "Gestion des personnels publics: évolution récentes et perspectives." Revue de l'IRES 53(1): 111-137.

DiMaggio, P. J. (1991). The new Institutionalism in organizational analysis. Chicago, University of Chicago Press.

Dolan, J. (2000). "The Senior Executive Service: Gender, Attitudes and Representative Bureaucracy." Journal of Public Administration Research and Theory 10(3): 513-529.

Dolan, J. A. and D. H. Rosenbloom (2003). Representative bureaucracy: Classic Readings and Continuing Controversies. New York, M.E. Sharpe.

du Gay, P., Ed. (2005). The Values of Bureaucracy. Oxford, Oxford University Press.

Dubar, C. and P. Tripier (2005). Sociologie des professions. Paris, Armand Colin.

Emery, Y. (2009). "L'apport du management de la qualité au renouveau du modèle bureaucratique." Revue de l'Innovation 14(3): 1-24.

Emery, Y. (2010). "Les réformes de l'administration publique en Suisse." Pyramides, revue du CERAP 19(1): 53-70.

Emery, Y. (2011). La gestion par les résultats dans les organisations publiques. La gouvernance. Frontières, dispositifs et agents. L. Côté. Québec, Presses de l'Université du Québec: 131-152.

Emery, Y. (2013). Gestion publique des ressources humaines. Introduction. Manuel d'administration publique suisse. A. Ladner, J.-L. Chappelet, Y. Emeryet al. Lausanne, Presses polytechniques et universitaires romandes: 446-459.

Emery, Y. (2013). Nouvelles politiques et processus de gestion publique des ressources humaines. Manuel d'administration publique suisse. A. Ladner, J.-L. Chappelet, Y. Emery et al. Lausanne, Presses polytechniques et universitaires romandes: 481-500.

Emery, Y. and D. Giauque (2005). Paradoxes de la gestion publique. Paris, L'Harmattan.

Emery, Y. and D. Giauque (2012). Motivations et valeurs des agents publics à l'épreuve des réformes. Laval, PUL.

Emery, Y., Giauque D., Rebmann F., (2014). The slow transformation of Swiss federal administrative elites. International Review of Administrative Sciences 80(4) pp. 687-708

Exworthy, M. and S. Halford, Eds. (1999). Professionals and the New Managerialism in the Public Sector. Buckingham, Open University Press.

Ferlie, E. and K. J. Geraghty (2007). Professionals in Public Services Organizations. Implications for Public Sector "reforming". The Oxford Handbook of Public Management. E. Ferlie, L. E. Lynn and C. Pollitt. Oxford, Oxford University Press: 422-445.

Frydman, B. (2013). Concilier le management avec les valeurs du judiciaire. Quel management pour quelle justice? T. D. Marchandise. Bruxelles, Larcier: 81-88.

Gaulejac de, V. (2005). La société malade de la gestion: idéologie gestionnaire, pouvoir managérial et harcèlement social. Paris, Seuil.

Giauque, D. (2006). "La domination, un concept incontournable pour la compréhension des phénomènes organisationnels." Revue économique et sociale(4): 51-64.

Giauque, D. and Y. Emery (2008). Repenser la gestion publique. Lausanne, Presses polytechniques et universitaires romandes.

Gillet-Goinard, F. and B. Seno (2011). Le grand livre du responsable qualité. Paris, Eyrolles/Editions d'Organisation.

Hablützel, P., T. Haldemann, et al. (1995). Umbruch in Politik und Verwaltung: Ansichten und Erfahrungen zum New Public Management in der Schweiz. Berne, Haupt.

Halford, S. and P. Leonard (1999). New Identities? Professionalism, managerialism and the construction of self. Professionals and the New Managerialism in the Public Sector. M. Exworthy and S. Halford. Buckingham, Open University Press.

Hamel, J. D. (2011). La "gestionnarisation" de la justice. Le nouveau management et l'indépendance des juges. B. Frydman and E. Jeuland. Paris, Dalloz: 131-140.

Hofstede, G. (1998). "Attitudes, values and organizational culture: disentangling the concepts." Organization Studies 19(3): 477.

Hufty, M., Ed. (1998). La pensée comptable. Etat, néolibéralisme, nouvelle gestion publique. Paris, PUF/Les nouveaux cahiers de l'IUED.

Jones, K. R. and R. W. Redman (2000). "Organizational Culture and Work Redesig: Experiences in Three Organizations." The Journal of Nursing Administration 30(12): 604-610.

Kessler, I., S. Bach, et al. (2007). "Comparing assistant roles in education and social care." International Journal of Human Resource Management 18(9): 1648-1666.

Kettiger, D. (2003). Wirkungsorientierte Verwaltungsführung in der Justiz. Bern, Société suisse des sciences administratives.

Kirkpatrick, I., S. Ackroyd, et al. (2005). The New Managerialism and Public Service Professions. Basingstoke, Palgrave McMillan.

Langbroek, P. (2005). Quality management concerning judges, judgements and court services. L'administration de la justice en Europe et l'évaluation de sa qualité. N. Rivero-Cabouat. Paris, France, Editions Montchrestien: 49-68.

Langbroek, P. (2008). "La réorganisation du système judiciaire des Pays-Bas." Revue française d'administration publique 125(1): 67-79.

Laufer, R. and A. Burlaud (1980). Management public, gestion et légitimité. Paris, Dalloz.

Lienhard, A. (2009). "Auch Richter sollen Rechenschaft ablegen." Unipress(1434): 17-18.

Lienhard, A. (2011). "New Public Management and Law: The Swiss Case." The NISPA Journal of Public Administration and Policy 4(2): 169-192.

Ludewig, R. (2008). Der Umgang mit dem richterlichen Ich-Ideal: Der Mensch hinter dem Richter. Der Richter und sein Bild. Wie sehen wir uns - wie werden wir gesehen? M. Heer. Bern, Stämpfli-Verlag: 25-44.

Ludewig, R., K. Weislehner, et al. (2007). Zwischen Recht und Gerechtigkeit - Richterinnen im Spiegel der Zeit. Bern, Stämpfli.

Mahon, P. and R. Schaller (2013). "Le système de réélection des juges: évidence démocratique ou épée de Damoclès?" Justice-Justiz-Giustizia(1).

Marchandise, T. D. (2013). Quel management pour quelle justice? Bruxelles, Larcier.

Martens, P. (2013). Le management modifie-t-il le rapport du juge à sa profession? Quel management pour quelle justice? T. D. Marchandise. Bruxelles, Larcier: 107-121.

Martineau, S. (2005). "L'observation en situation: enjeux, possibilités et limites." Recherches qualitatives Hors Série(2): 5-17.

Mayo, E. (1933). The human problems of an industrial civilization. Boston.

Mintzberg, H. (1982). Structure et dynamique des organisations. Paris, Les Editions d'Organisation.

Norman, R. (2007). Pièges de la gestion des performances et gouvernance du secteur public. Dilemmes de la GRH publique. Y. Emery and D. Giauque. Lausanne, LEP.

Normann, R. (1994). Le management des services. Paris, InterEditions.

Ostrom, B., R. Hanson, et al. (2005). "Court Cultures and Their Consequences." The Court Manager 20(1): 14-23.

Perry, J. L. and W. Vandenabeele (2008). Behavioral Dynamics: Institutions, Identities and Self-Regulation. Motivation in Public Management. J. L. Perry and A. Hondeghem. New York, Oxford University Press: 56-79.

Peters, T. and R. H. Waterman (1982). In search of Excellence: lessons from America's best-run companies. New-York, Harper and Row.

Poltier, E. (2012). "Le pouvoir judiciaire "s'administre lui-même"." Richterzeitung.

Pümpin, C., J. M. Kobi, et al. (1985). "Unternehmenskultur." Die Orientierung, Schweizerische Volksbank 85.

Robert, A. D. and A. Bouillaguet (2002). L'analyse de contenu. Paris, PUF.

Rouban, L. (2007). Les systèmes d'incitation entre cultures nationales et régulations professionnelles. Dilemmes de la GRH publique. Y. Emery and D. Giauque. Lausanne, LEP: 161-186.

Schedler, K. and I. Proeller, Eds. (2007). Cultural Aspects of Public Management Reform. Oxford, UK, Elsevier.

Schein, E. (1971). Psychologie et organisations. Paris, Hommes et techniques.

Schneider, B., Ed. (1990). Organizational climate and culture. San Francisco, Jossey-Bass.

Sehested, K. (2002). "How new public management reforms challenge the roles of professionnals." International Journal of Public Administration 25(12): 1513-1537.

Strauss, A. and J. Corbin (2004). Les fondements de la recherche qualitative: techniques et procédures de développement de la théorie enracinée. Fribourg, Academic Press Fribourg.

Thoenig, J.-C. (2000). L'aventure des réformes administratives est aussi une affaire de professionnalisme. L'administration dans tous ses états. Y. Emery Lausanne, Presses polytechniques et universitaires romandes: 163-173.

Vigour, C. (2006). "Justice: l'introduction d'une rationalité managériale comme euphémisation des enjeux politiques." Droit et Société 63(2): 425-455.

Watzlawick, P., J. Weakland, et al. (1975). Changements: paradoxes et psychothérapie. Paris, Norton, Seuil.

Weber, M. (1971). Economie et société. Paris, Plon.

Wipfli, H. (2006). Justizmanagement am Beispiel eines Steuergerichts: Struktur, Organisation und Führung Master thesis, Universität Bern.

Richter führen – ist es möglich, und wie? Chancen und Herausforderungen bei der direkten Personalführung der Richterinnen und Richter

Autoren

Vera Hertig, Institut de hautes études en administration publique, Université de Lausanne

Prof. Dr. Yves Emery, Professeur ordinaire, Management public et gestion des ressources humaines, Institut de hautes études en administration publique, Université de Lausanne

Abstract

Das letzte Kapitel des Buches stellt die Frage zum Management der Richter noch konkreter, in dem die Chancen und Herausforderungen detailliert werden, die mit der Führung der Magistraten in dieser Schlüsselrolle im Herzen der Justiz einhergehen. Von der vielfach verbreiteten Bestätigung der Literatur, nach der ein wirksames und unternehmerisches Leadership eine Grundvoraussetzung für eine effiziente Justiz ist, fokalisiert sich die Studie auf die direkte Führung der Magistraten und beschäftigt sich daher nicht mit der politischen Führung (obere Aufsicht der Justiz). Sie durchleuchtet zunächst die reichliche Literatur zum Thema Leadership im Allgemeinen und spezifischer zum Thema Leadership innerhalb der öffentlichen Organisationen, der professionellen Bürokratien (so wie Gerichte oder Spitäler) und der Justiz. Als Synthese fasst die Studie folgende Schlüsselfragen zusammen: wer kann die Richter führen? Auf welche Verantwortlichkeiten sollte diese Führung zielen? Wie soll man vorgehen, und warum? Auf dieser Basis analysieren die Autoren die Aussagen der Richter sowie die anderer zentraler Akteure in der Justiz (interne und externe, so wie politische Verantwortliche, Rechtsanwälte und Journalisten) aus 56 halb-strukturierten Interviews. Daraus ergibt sich, dass die Führung der Richter nur ein Erfolg sein kann, wenn sie die professionelle Kultur der Richter respektiert. Um das zu erreichen, formulieren und diskutieren die Autoren einige provokante Thesen hinsichtlich der Führung der Richter, zum Beispiel die Tatsache, dass Richter nicht geführt werden können, weil sie keine Vorgesetzen haben. Daraus ergibt sich, dass ein informeller und kollegialer Führungsstil sicher wünschenswert wäre, aber nicht ausreichend ist: eine Struktur sowie eine minimale Führung würde Klarheit in die aktuelle Situation bringen, aber es würde von Seiten der betroffenen Personen in dieser Rolle echte Führungsqualitäten erfordern, und einen partizipativen Führungsstil, der eher transformational und instrumental als transaktional sein sollte.

1. Einleitung

150 Im Kontext der Modernisierung des öffentlichen Sektors und des in den 1990er aufkommenden Paradigmas des New Public Management (NPM) werden in der öffentlichen Verwaltung vermehrt die Funktionsweisen und die Managementinstrumente des privaten Sektors übernommen und angewendet.[1] Diese aktuelle Diskussion hat sowohl auf kantonaler wie auch auf Bundesebene zu Reformen der Schweizer Justiz geführt.[2] Gefordert werden eine strengere Ressourcenverwaltung, Budget-Restriktionen, eine erhöhte Transparenz gegenüber den beteiligten Parteien, eine Steigerung der Qualität der Leistungserbringung sowie die Einführung von Leistungskontrollen und Rechenschaftspflicht gegenüber den Kontrollinstanzen[3] Im Zuge der Modernisierungswelle NPM sind aufgrund des höheren Leistungs- und Effizienzdrucks Themen wie die Führung an Gerichten vermehrt in den Fokus gerückt.[4] Dies führt im Umfeld der Justiz zu einer Entwicklung von einer sehr rechtlich geprägten Kultur zu einer mehr und mehr unternehmerisch geprägten Kultur.[5] Während sich die rechtliche Kultur durch den Respekt der Verfahrensprozesse, die hierarchische Loyalität und den Vorrang der Gleichbehandlung auszeichnen, ist die unternehmerische Kultur geprägt durch einen Leadership öffentlicher Manager, Risikofreudigkeit, Output-Orientation, Konkurrenzdenken und Innovationsgewinn.[6] Da sich diese Management-Werte von den traditionellen Charakteristiken der Justiz unterscheiden, stellt sich die Frage, ob diese neuen managementorientierten Führungsansätze mit dem Umfeld der Dritten Gewalt kompatibel sind.

151 Zuerst einmal ist die organisationale, administrative Führung von der politischen Führung abzugrenzen. In diesem Kapitel wird die administrative Führung des direkten Vorgesetzten, also des nicht-politischen Kopfes

---

1 VIGODA-GADOT/MEIRI (2008), GIAUQUE/EMERY (2008).

2 KETTIGER (2003), LIENHARD et al. (2005).

3 POLTIER (2012/3).

4 KETTIGER, 2003, S. 187.

5 EMERY/DE SANTIS (2014).

6 DENHARDT/ DENHARDT (2003), SCHEDLER/PROELLER (2007).

der Organisation untersucht. Das Thema des personenorientierten Leaderships ist ein beliebtes Forschungsfeld, wobei gerade dem spezifischen Bereich des öffentlichen Dienstes im Gegensatz zum privaten Sektor eher wenig Aufmerksamkeit zuteilwird. Dies gilt umso mehr für den Kontext der Justiz und die Führung von Richterinnen und Richtern. Leadership wird in der Literatur als wichtiger Einflussfaktor für die Leistung der Organisation sowie die Leistung und Zufriedenheit der Mitarbeiter beurteilt.[7] In der Justiz besteht jedoch eine gewisse Uneinigkeit über die Bedeutung eines solchen Leaderships. Kettiger[8] kommt in einem Workshop mit Richtern zum Schluss, dass kein wirklicher Konsens zur Frage nach Umfang, Ausgestaltung und Verantwortung der Führung im Gericht besteht. Es handelt sich um ein kontroverses Thema, das mehr Aufmerksamkeit durch die Forschung verdient.

Einerseits herrscht die Meinung, dass eine gute Personalführung mit geeigneten Führungsinstrumenten eine unverzichtbare Bedingung darstellt für eine wirkungsorientierte und effizient verwaltete Justiz, welche eine gute Qualität an Rechtsprechung erbringt.[9] Gemäss Kettiger[10] liegt es im Interesse der Richterschaft und der Justiz im Allgemeinen, wenn auf die Wahrnehmung einer formellen Führung gedrängt wird. Gerade hinsichtlich der Entwicklung einer privatwirtschaftlich geprägten Kultur im öffentlichen Sektor sprechen Holmes und Shand[11] der unmittelbaren Führung durch geeignete Führungskräfte eine wichtige Rolle zu. Diese hat die zentrale Aufgabe, den Wandel zu begünstigen und zu leiten. Die Forschung von Wice[12] hat gezeigt, dass lokale Führungsprozesse eine wichtige Voraussetzung sind für das Gelingen von Justizreformen. Dies beinhaltet schlussendlich auch die Sicherstellung einer effizienten Führung von Richtern als Kernakteure des Gerichts. 152

Andererseits stellt die Einführung neuer Führungskompetenzen auch ein sensibles Thema dar, welches schnell auf Widerstand bei der Richterschaft stosst. Dies veranschaulicht das aktuelle Beispiel der Strafgerichtsbarkeit in Genf, wo im Rahmen eines Reformprojektes eine stärkere Zentralisierung der Kompetenzen auf den Generalstaatsanwalt enormen Wi- 153

---

[7] VAN WART (2003).
[8] KETTIGER (2003).
[9] WIPFLI (2006).
[10] KETTIGER (2003), S. 155.
[11] HOLMES/SHAND (1995).
[12] WICE (1995).

derstand eines Grossteils der Richter auslöste. Die Richter argumentierten gegen diese als Machtkonzentration und Hierarchisierung empfundene Reform, da sie, so ihre Argumentation, der Justizkultur widerspreche und die richterliche Unabhängigkeit gefährde. Zudem werden Führungsaufgaben oftmals nicht als gleichwertige Aufgabe angesehen wie die Rechtsprechung (siehe Emery/de Santis, Kapitel 2). Dies gilt insbesondere für Richter, welche zwar teilweise mit Führungsfunktionen betraut sind, aber sich kaum mit Führungsfragen auseinandersetzen.[13]

154 Das vorliegende Kapitel identifiziert die berufliche Kultur der Richter als wichtigen Faktor, welcher das Konzept der direkten Personalführung von Richtern mit besonderen Herausforderungen konfrontiert. Laut Bouckaert[14] beeinflussen die Einstellungen, Werte und Verhaltensweisen der Richter als Kernakteure der Justiz aufgrund ihrer Dominanz die gesamte Funktionsweise der Organisation. Eine so stark geprägte Berufskultur kann ein bedeutsames Hindernis für die Einführung neuer Managementkonzepte darstellen.[15] Es stellt sich die Frage, welche Widersprüche aber auch Entwicklungsmöglichkeiten sich durch die Einführung einer managementorientierten Führungskultur im Zusammentreffen mit der durch Unabhängigkeit, Autonomie und Individualismus geprägten richterlichen Berufskultur ergeben.

155 Ziel des Kapitels ist es, die Chancen und Herausforderungen der direkten Personalführung von Richtern auf Basis von persönlichen Erfahrungen, Meinungen, Vorstellungen und Werte der Justizakteure zu identifizieren. Untersucht wird die Frage, ob und welche personenbezogenen Führungsmodelle mit der beruflichen Kultur der Richter kompatibel sind. Die Personalführung inhaltlich zu definieren oder ein konkretes Modell für die Führung von Richtern vorzuschlagen, würde das Ausmass dieses Artikels sprengen. Jedoch soll die Arbeit erste Hinweise zu den Chancen und Grenzen der Umsetzung einer direkten Personalführung von Richtern liefern. Daher lautet die Forschungsfrage: Richter führen – Ist es möglich und wie? Welches sind die Chancen und Herausforderungen für die direkte Personalführung von Richtern?

156 Das Kapitel liefert zuerst eine Zusammenfassung der Literatur mit einem Einblick in die wichtigsten Personalführungsansätze und Erkenntnis-

13 KETTIGER (2003), S. 154.
14 BOUCKAERT (2007).
15 VIGOUR (2008).

se der Leadership-Forschung. Ein Fokus liegt auf der Frage nach Leadership im öffentlichen Sektor, in professionellen Bürokratien und in der Justiz selbst. Im Anschluss an die Literatur-Besprechung werden die in den geführten Interviews genannten, zentralen Argumente zur Führung von Richtern zusammengefasst. Abschliessend wird eine Analyse der Aussagen der Justizakteure vorgenommen. Die Charakteristiken der beruflichen Kultur der Richter und ihr Zusammenhang zur direkten Personalführung werden aufgezeigt sowie an Hand provokativer Hypothesen die Chancen und Grenzen einer solchen Führung diskutiert. Das Kapitel stützt sich auf die Analyse einer Serie von halbstrukturierten Interviews (56), welche im Rahmen eines grösseren Forschungsprojektes an erst- sowie zweitinstanzlichen Gerichten in zwei Deutschschweizer Kantonen, allen Welschschweizer Kantonen sowie dem Tessin durchgeführt wurden. Befragt wurden sowohl interne Justizakteure wie Richter, Gerichtsschreiber, Generalsekretäre und Justizmanager sowie externe Akteure wie Politiker, Anwälte und Journalisten (siehe Punkt 3 für mehr Details zur Methode).

2. Literatur

2.1 Personalführung und Leadership

Im Kapitel wird im Folgenden von Personalführung im engeren 157
Sinne ausgegangen. Darunter fällt die unmittelbare, interpersonelle Führung der Mitarbeiter durch einen Vorgesetzten mit einem bestimmten Führungsstil und unter Anwendung von Führungsinstrumenten, mit dem Ziel der Beeinflussung und Verhaltensänderung der Mitarbeiter. Es handelt sich demnach um eine zielorientierte und soziale Einflussnahme zur Erfüllung gemeinsamer Arbeitsaufgaben in einer strukturierten Arbeitssituation.[16] Diese direkte Funktion der Personalführung hat zur Aufgabe, die fünf zentralen Personalprozesse (Personalgewinnung, -Beurteilung, -Einsatz und -Erhaltung sowie die Personalentwicklung und Freistellung) umzusetzen und insbesondere die Aktivierung der Mitarbeitermotivation und Leistungsbereitschaft sicherzustellen.[17]

16 KOLB (2008).
17 THOM/RITZ (2000).

158 Die Forschung über die Natur der unterschiedlichen Personalführungsansätze und ihren Einfluss auf den Führungserfolg wird in der Literatur unter dem Begriff des Leaderships behandelt. Wie Stogdill treffend formuliert:[18] „There are as many definitions of leadership as there are persons who have attempted to define the concept“. Gemäss der Leadership-Definition von Peter F. Drucker[19] ist das wichtigste Element für das Vorhandensein einer Führung, dass sie bei den Mitarbeitern Gefolgschaft findet: „The only definition of a leader is someone who has followers”. Es scheint ein Konsens darüber zu bestehen, dass Leadership einer der wichtigsten Faktoren ist, welcher die organisationale Effektivität und Effizienz sowie die Leistung und Zufriedenheit der einzelnen Mitarbeiter beeinflusst.[20] Ein effektives Leadership schafft im Idealfall Produkte oder Dienstleistungen von besserer Qualität, einen effizienteren Service, fördert den Personalzusammenhalt und die -Entwicklung und erhöht die Arbeitszufriedenheit, die Motivation und das organisationale Engagement der Mitarbeiter. Auch stellt es der Organisation eine weitergehende Zielführung und Vision zur Verfügung, sorgt für eine optimale Verbindung der Organisation an die Umwelt, fördert die Innovation und stärkt die organisationale Kultur[21]. Dies verdeutlicht die Vielfältigkeit der Rolle und des Mehrwerts eines Leaders in einer Organisation. Doch wie lässt sich eine effektive, direkte Personalführung definieren und schlussendlich umsetzen?

159 Neuere Konzepte der Personalführungsforschung betonen, dass effektives Leadership nicht nur von den persönlichen Eigenschaften des Leaders abhängt (Theorie des „grossen Mannes“, sog. Trait-based Theory).[22] Direkte Führung kann nicht allein erfasst werden mit angeborenen, personellen Eigenschaften oder eindeutigen Rollenzuteilungen. Vielmehr zeigt sie sich in der nicht-linearen Beziehung zwischen dem Leader zu seinen Followern, welche in ständiger Interaktion zueinander stehen und sich gegenseitig beeinflussen.[23] Die moderne Forschung konzentriert sich folglich nicht nur auf die Verhaltensweise und Eigenschaften des Leaders, sondern auch auf die Mitarbeiter und die konkrete Situation. Die sog.

---

18 STOGDILL (1974), S. 7.
19 DRUCKER (1998), S. XI.
20 VAN WART (2003), BROUSSINE (2003), S. 176.
21 VAN WART (2003).
22 BIRD (1940), COMMISSION (2013), S. 8, JENKINS (1947).
23 SOHM (2007), S. 3.

„Situational- und Contingency-Theories“[24] fragen nach der Vereinbarkeit des Führungsverhaltens, also dem konkreten Verhalten des Vorgesetzten in einer bestimmten Situation, mit dem internen Kontext der Organisation. Der kontextabhängige Ansatz dient noch heute oftmals als Basis von Leadership-Theorien.[25] Die Hauptannahme ist, dass ein Führungsverhalten sich je nach Kontext flexibel an die jeweilige Situation anpassen muss, um das gewünschte Outcome erreichen zu können.[26] Als relevanter Faktor für den Führungserfolg wird die Anpassung des Führungsverhaltens an die Eigenschaften der konkreten Situation, der Aufgabe und der zu führenden Mitarbeiter definiert (siehe bspw. situationsgebundener Ansatz von Campell, Marvin, Lawler, & Weick).[27] Weiter stellt sich die Frage nach dem geeigneten Führungsstil, womit ein dauerhaftes, immer wieder zu beobachtendes Verhaltensmuster und die dazugehörige Grundeinstellung des Vorgesetzten gemeint ist.[28] Ein wichtiger Aspekt der interpersonellen Führung ist die Frage nach dem Ausmass der Mitwirkung der Mitarbeiter an der Führung.[29] So besagt der partizipativ-situative Führungsstil, dass ein Vorgesetzter seine Mitarbeiter so stark wie möglich, aber nicht mehr als nötig in die Entscheidungsbildung einbeziehen soll, je nachdem wie die Situation, der Zeitdruck, die Aufgabe sowie die Kenntnisse, Fähigkeiten und der Wille zur Mitwirkung der Mitarbeiter ausgestaltet sind.[30] Die ideale Mischung zu finden aus Mitwirkung der Mitarbeiter, Zentralisierung oder Dezentralisierung von Entscheidungskompetenzen, zwischen einem eher partizipatorischen oder autoritärem Führungsstil, ist gemäss Van Wart[31] eine der grössten Herausforderungen moderner Führungskräfte.

Ein bedeutender Prozess in der Forschung der Führungsstile ist die in 160
den 1980er vorgenommene Abgrenzung von transaktionaler Führung, welche auf Belohnung und Zwang basiert, zu der bisher vernachlässigten transformationalen Führung mit visionären, emotionalen und Wertebasierten Elementen.[32] Diese Unterscheidung verdeutlicht die Abgrenzung

---

24 COMMISSION (2013), S. 8 ff.
25 VAN WART (2003), BROUSSINE (2003), S. 179.
26 COMMISSION (2013).
27 CAMPELL/MARVIN/LAWLER/WEICK (1979).
28 KOLB (2008), S. 384 f.
29 VROOM/JAGO (1988).
30 DUBS (2005).
31 VAN WART (2013).
32 VAN WART (2003).

von Leadership zu Management.[33] Laut der OECD dreht sich Leadership im Gegensatz zum Management um „informal influence – how to mobilize people through values and visions“.[34] Oder anders gesagt: „Leadership shapes the future; management delivers it“.[35] Die managementorientierte, transaktionale Führung konzentriert sich auf die tägliche Interaktion des Leaders mit den Geführten auf operativem Niveau mithilfe von Zielvereinbarung, Leistungskontrollen, Leistungskorrekturen und das Zurückgreifen auf finanzielle Anreize. Gemäss Antonakis[36] funktioniert transaktionales Leadership jedoch gerade in unsicheren und krisenähnlichen Situationen nicht optimal und ist limitiert in seiner Funktion, die Mitarbeiter für die Ziele der Organisation zu mobilisieren. Demgegenüber steht beim transformationalen Leadership die Führung von organisationalem Wandel und die Bereitstellung von Vision, Kultur und Werten im Vordergrund.[37] Dabei wird vom symbolischen und charismatischen Leader die Kommunikation einer interessanten Vision erwartet, welche den zu erledigenden Aufgaben einen tiefergehenden Sinn zuweist. Die Vision soll mit den Werten und der Kultur der Organisation, der Mitarbeiter und des Umfeldes verbunden werden und dem Personal so eine intrinsische und inspirierende Motivation bereitstellen.[38] Zentral dabei ist die Entwicklung von Mitarbeiter-Fähigkeiten und Potenzialen sowie die Schaffung eines gemeinsamen Bewusstseins für die Ziele der Organisation. „Transformational leaders shift goals (of followers) away from personal, safety and security towards achievement, self-actualization and the greater good“.[39] Effektiv ist ein Leader dann, wenn er seine Follower beeinflussen kann und sich diese mit dem Leader selbst, seiner Vision und seinen Zielen identifizieren und ihm ihr Vertrauen schenken.[40] Als wichtig für die organisationale und individuelle Leistung identifiziert Antonakis schliesslich das instrumentelle Leadership. Dieses beinhaltet die Konkretisierung der Vision in strategische und taktische Pläne und die Förderung und Begleitung der Mitarbeiter bei der Erfüllung ihrer Leistungsziele in Form von

---

33 Broussine (2003), S. 185.
34 OECD (2001) S. 15.
35 Broussine (2003), S. 180.
36 Antonakis (2006), S. 6.
37 Hill (2006), S. 82.
38 Orazi/Turrini/Valotti (2013), S. 529 f.
39 Bass (1998), S. 41.
40 Antonakis (2006), S. 9.

Monitoring der Zielerfüllung und Bereitstellen von konstruktivem Feedback.[41]

Die Forschung hat erkannt, dass sich mit geeigneten Persönlichkeitsmerkmalen und einer formellen Autorität alleine kein interpersoneller Führungserfolg beschreiben lässt. Effektive Führung wird vielmehr dadurch gekennzeichnet, dass sich die aufgrund der Persönlichkeit ergebenden Verhaltensweisen der Führungskraft mit der spezifischen Situation, d.h. mit den Kompetenzen des Leaders, den Eigenschaften der Situation, der Aufgaben sowie der zu führenden Personen vereinbaren lassen.[42] Zudem basiert ein vollständiger Leadership-Ansatz nicht nur auf Belohnung, Sanktion und Zwangsgewalt (transaktionales Leadership), sondern schliesst auch die Kommunikation einer Vision, Werte und Ziele mit ein. Die Mitarbeiter sollen sich mit diesen identifizieren können und sie damit inspirieren, motivieren und engagieren (transformationales Leadership). Weiter ist es notwendig, die Vision in strategische Pläne zu konkretisieren und die Mitarbeiter bei der Erfüllung ihrer Leistungsziele konstruktiv zu unterstützen (instrumentelles Leadership). Im Folgenden soll geklärt werden, welchen Mehrwert die drei genannten Führungsansätze für die direkte Führung von Richtern generieren und welcher am besten mit der komplexen Situation der Justiz und der Richter vereinbar ist. 161

2.2 Personalführung und Leadership im öffentlichen Sektor

Hier handelt es sich um die zentrale Frage, ob sich Leadership im öffentlichen Sektor von demjenigen des privaten Sektors unterscheidet. Existiert ein Leadership-Modell eigens für den öffentlichen Sektor oder werden Leadership-Modelle des privaten Sektors angewandt? Die Forschung, welche Leadership im öffentlichen Sektor untersucht, gestaltet sich längst nicht so umfangreich wie diejenige des privaten Sektors.[43] Erst mit der Welle der Modernisierung der öffentlichen Verwaltung im Rahmen der wirkungsorientierten Verwaltungsführung steigerte sich auch das Interesse an der Funktion und der Ausgestaltung der Führung. Eine Untersuchung der Führungskultur in NPM-Projekten zeigt, dass die Personalführung und insbesondere der Aspekt der Personalentwicklung während 162

41 ANTONAKIS (2006), S. 13.
42 DUBS (2005).
43 ORAZI et al. (2013), S. 523.

den Reformprojekten einen grossen Bedeutungswandel durchlebten und danach einen höheren Stellenwert besassen.[44] Mit der Einführung des NPM in der öffentlichen Verwaltung soll gemäss Schedler und Proeller eine weitreichende Veränderung des Führungsverständnisses erreicht werden. Während in der Karikatur der klassischen Bürokratie die Führung weitgehend rechtlich vorgeschriebenen Verfahren und Vorschriften überlassen wird und „gute" Vorgesetzte weder positive noch negative Einflüsse entfalten, soll mithilfe des NPM die Bedeutung der Führung durch Vorgesetzte betont, d.h. gute Führung belohnt und schlechte Führung vermehrt sanktioniert werden.[45] Im Idealfall, so die Autoren, werde Führung nicht mehr primär aus der Kontrolle rechtlicher Verfahrensvorschriften bestehen, sondern in der Förderung und Kontrolle der strategischen Ziele der öffentlichen Verwaltung. Führungskräfte stellen dabei nicht primär Kontrolleure von Sachaufgaben dar. Sie sind vielmehr eine Art Coach, oder Steward, welche die Mitarbeiter motivieren und ihren Erfolg erst ermöglichen.[46]

163 Erst ab den 1990er Jahren kann man von einem vom privaten Sektor autonomen Forschungsbereich des „Public Leadership" sprechen, auch wenn die Debatte immer noch in den Anfängen steht.[47] Als möglicher Grund für die frühere Vernachlässigung wird unter anderem der weitverbreitete Glauben verantwortlich gemacht, dass der öffentliche Sektor durch mächtige, politische Kräfte geführt und beeinflusst wird, welche nicht in der Kontrolle von administrativen Führungskräften liegen. Deshalb die Annahme, dass administratives Leadership keinen grossen Beitrag an die öffentliche Organisation leisten kann.[48] Leadership wird im Umfeld der öffentlichen Verwaltung manchmal sogar als zu politisch wahrgenommen. Der Begriff löst so teilweise sogar Angst vor unerlaubtem Ermessen und unkontrollierbarer Autorität und Machtkonzentration aus. Daher gibt es auch Autoren, welche die Legitimität des Leaderships im öffentlichen Sektor an sich in Frage stellen.[49] Dennoch erkannte die Forschung in den letzten Jahrzehnten, dass ein geeignetes Leadership sich auch im öffentlichen Sektor positiv auf die Leistung und Motivation der

---

44 KLAGES (1998).
45 SCHEDLER/PROELLER (2009), S. 234.
46 SCHEDLER/PROELLER (2009), S. 235.
47 ORAZI et al. (2013), S. 533.
48 VAN WART (2003), S. 215.
49 FAIRHOLM (2004), S. 578.

Mitarbeiter sowie die Innovationsfähigkeit der gesamten Organisation auswirkt, auch wenn andere, bspw. kontextuelle Faktoren, einen grösseren oder genauso grossen Einfluss haben.[50] Studien zeigen unter anderem auf, dass ein transformationaler Leadership-Stil, welcher den Handlungs- und Ermessensspielraum bei Mitarbeitern erhöht, gerade bei anspruchsvollen Aufgaben einen positiven Einfluss auf die Leistung hat. Park und Rainey[51] haben in ihrer Studie festgestellt, dass ein Leadership, welches sich der Belohnung intrinsischer Motivation bedient, Versetzungs- oder Kündigungsabsichten verkleinert sowie die individuelle Leistung und Arbeitszufriedenheit erhöht. Leadership, so Fairholm,[52] sei heute ein unverzichtbarer Aspekt der öffentlichen Verwaltung.

Je mehr sich die Forschenden zu den allgemein gültigen Eigenschaften des Public Leaderships einigen, desto mehr werden die Unterschiede zum privatwirtschaftlichen Sektor betont.[53] Solche Unterschiede findet man bspw. aufgrund der unterschiedlichen Herausforderungen, mit denen der öffentliche Sektor konfrontiert ist. Moderne Führungskräfte in der öffentlichen Verwaltung müssen sich mit der durchregulierten rechtlichen Struktur, den sich teilweise widersprechende öffentlichen Erwartungen und Zielsetzungen, den sich vom privaten Sektor unterscheidenden Werten und Kultur, dem marktwirtschaftlichen Einfluss von gekürzten Ressourcen und höherem Leistungsfokus, dem offeneren und kritischeren Diskurs in der Öffentlichkeit sowie dem verstärkten politischen Einfluss auseinandersetzen.[54] Zudem besitzen Führungskräfte im öffentlichen Sektor oftmals nicht die entsprechenden Befugnisse, um das Personal eigenhändig zu kündigen, zu rekrutieren, zu befördern oder ihr Gehalt festzulegen. Weiter gibt es Untersuchungen, die zeigen, dass Mitarbeiter im öffentlichen Sektor sich in ihrer Motivationsstruktur von denjenigen des privaten Dienstes unterscheiden[55]. So sollen sie sich durch ein höheres Niveau der Public Service Motivation auszeichnen und daher stärker durch altruistische Motive und weniger durch finanzielle Anreize motiviert werden.[56] 164

---

[50] ORAZI et al. (2013), S. 531.
[51] PARK/RAINEY (2008).
[52] FAIRHOLM (2004), S. 577.
[53] ORAZI et al. (2013), S. 533.
[54] VAN WART (2013), S. 3, HILL (2006), S. 82.
[55] EMERY/GIAUQUE (2012).
[56] ORAZI et al. (2013), S. 527 f.

165 Doch welcher Führungsstil ist nun angemessen für den öffentlichen Sektor? Laut Orazi et al.[57] sollen Führungskräfte in der Ausführung ihrer Aufgaben vor allem die Erhaltung ihrer moralischen Integrität und die Beachtung öffentlicher Werte sicherstellen. Die Hauptannahme ist, dass der Führungserfolg dabei mehr auf gemeinsamen, von der Führungskraft vorgelebten und kommunizierten, Werten und Zielen basiert als auf organisationaler Autorität und Kontrolle.[58] In Anlehnung an die Definition der Führungsstile durch Antonakis[59] scheint der transformationale Leadership im Kontext des öffentlichen Sektors geeigneter zu sein als der, auf Zwang und hierarchischen Beziehungen basierende, transaktionale Leadership. Auch Kellis und Ran[60] beurteilen den traditionellen, transaktionalen Leadership als nicht effektiv für das komplexe Umfeld öffentlicher Organisationen. Sie plädieren in ihrer Studie für den Einsatz eines modernen Leadership-Ansatzes. Dieser kombiniert sowohl Aspekte der moralischen Integrität und Werte der Führungskraft mit dem Willen, die Führungsverantwortung unter verschiedenen internen und externen Stakeholdern aufzuteilen (sog. „distributed, shared leadership") und der Fähigkeit, die Mitarbeiter für die organisationalen Ziele effektiv zu motivieren und engagieren.[61] Schedler und Proeller[62] schreiben zudem dem persönlichen Leistungsfeedback eine wichtige Rolle zu, da den Mitarbeitern sonst die Grundlage für einen selbständigen Erfolg fehle. Das Instrument des ständig kritisch-unterstützenden Feedbacks ist laut Antonakis[63] ein zentraler Aspekt der instrumentellen Führung.

166 Als wichtig für die zukünftige Forschung des „Public leadership" bewerten Orazi et al.[64], dass die Besonderheiten des öffentlichen Dienstes vermehrt in Betracht gezogen und nicht einfach die Modelle des privaten Sektors kopiert werden. Gleiches gilt für die Justiz und umso mehr für die Führung von Richtern. So können nicht einfach Leadership-Modelle aus einem anderen Kontext übernommen werden, ohne die rechtliche Strukturierung sowie die spezifische Kultur der Richter miteinzubeziehen. Die Forschung zu „Public Leadership" lässt die Vermutung zu, dass auch bei

---

[57] ORAZI et al. (2013), S. 522.
[58] FAIRHOLM (2004), S. 580.
[59] ANTONAKIS/LIDEN (2009).
[60] KELLIS/RAN (2012).
[61] KELLIS/RAN (2012), S. 138.
[62] SCHEDLER/PROELLER (2009), S. 235.
[63] ANTONAKIS/LIDEN (2009), S. 9.
[64] ORAZI et al. (2013), S. 534 f.

der direkten Führung von Richtern ein besonderer Fokus auf moderne Führungsaspekte im Sinne des transformationalen und instrumentellen Leaderships gelegt werden sollte.

2.3 Führung in professionellen Bürokratien

In Bezug auf Organisationen mit ähnlichen Eigenschaften wie die Justiz lässt sich am ehesten auf professionelle Bürokratien gemäss der Typologie von Mintzberg[65] verweisen. Solche Organisationen sind dadurch charakterisiert, dass ihre Kernaktivität von einer Berufskategorie mit dominanter beruflichen Kultur, also Lehrer, Professoren, Ärzte oder eben Richter getragen werden.[66] Die Berufskultur der Kernakteure, welche allesamt einer hochqualifizierten Berufskategorie angehören und auf der operativen Ebene tätig sind, beeinflusst aufgrund ihrer Dominanz die gesamte Funktionsweise der Organisation. Eine so stark ausgeprägte Berufskultur kann sich als Hindernis für die Entwicklung von Management manifestieren, da neue Führungsansätze sowie Führungskultur im Allgemeinen als bedrohlich für die festgeschriebenen beruflichen Regeln und Werte gewertet werden.[67] Bevor im nächsten Abschnitt die Führung von Richtern thematisiert wird, macht es Sinn, einen Blick auf Erkenntnisse zur Führungskultur in anderen professionellen Bürokratien wie der Schule oder des Spitals zu werfen. 167

Im Kontext der Schule wird häufig die Befürchtung genannt, dass ein Führungskonzept die stärkere Hierarchisierung der Organisation zur Folge hat, was diese mit zusätzlichen Verwaltungsarbeiten belastet und die Lehrer von ihrer Kernaufgabe ablenkt.[68] Häufig wird die Auffassung geteilt, dass demokratische Gruppenentscheidungen immer besser seien als Entscheidungen durch nur eine einzelne Führungsperson. Diese werden deshalb eher als Moderator statt als Führungspersönlichkeit mit echten Entscheidungskompetenzen wahrgenommen.[69] Dubs gibt zu bedenken, dass diese Ängste meist von einem überholten Führungsbegriff herrühren und die zunehmende Komplexität der Organisation unterschätzt wird. Ein oftmals angesprochenes Thema im Spital ist der zu starre und einseitige 168

---

[65] MINTZBERG (1982).
[66] BOUCKAERT (2007).
[67] KIRKPATRICK et al. (2005), VIGOUR (2008).
[68] DUBS (2005), S. 21.
[69] DUBS (2005), S. 127.

Fokus auf technische Kenntnisse und Fähigkeiten. Der Hauptteil der Ressourcen wird in professionellen Bürokratien in die Aneignung von technischen Kompetenzen gesteckt, und Ressourcen für Feedback zu Führungsverhalten und Teamarbeit werden vernachlässigt.[70] Oft werden nur Personen in Führungspositionen akzeptiert, welche ein fachliches Wissen und Können und daher ein zwingend notwendiges „erfahrenes Problemverständnis" aufweisen. Managementkompetenzen spielen eher eine untergeordnete Rolle.[71] Dies kann dazu führen, dass Führungskräfte Fähigkeiten vermissen lassen, die sie dazu befähigen, Mitarbeiter zu motivieren, Teamarbeit zu fördern oder Konflikte zu managen.[72] Manchmal fehlt bei leitenden Ärzten ganz die Einsicht, dass Personalführung nicht nur Aufgabe der administrativen Personalabteilung ist, sondern eine nicht delegierbare Verantwortung jeder Führungskraft.[73] Bei der Führung von Lehrern oder Ärzten wird häufig ein kooperativer und partizipativer Führungsstil gefordert. Dies gilt insbesondere für medizinische wie pädagogische Aufgabenbereiche, wo die Berufskollegen über genauso viel Expertenwissen verfügen und mit ihren Kenntnissen und Erfahrungen etwas zur Lösung beitragen können und wollen. Dubs[74] betont aber auch, dass trotz des partizipativen Führungsstils dennoch ein Entscheid des Vorgesetzten möglich sein muss, wenn die Mitwirkung zu keinem Konsens führt.

169 Eine zentrale Befürchtung ist, dass die Einführung neuer Management-Funktionen und -Logiken die Werte und Kultur des traditionellen Berufsstandes verdrängt. Byrkjeflot und Jespersen kommen in ihrer Studie über öffentliche Spitäler jedoch zum Schluss, dass Management-Reformen den traditionellen Berufsstand nicht verdrängen oder dessen Autonomie bedrohen. Vielmehr existieren in der Praxis unterschiedliche Typen von „hybrid management", welche aus der Verschmelzung der Logiken und Werten beider Berufskategorien entstehen. „Hybrid Manager" scheinen mit Management-Reformen auf unterschiedliche, sehr kreative Weise umzugehen, so dass sie ihre Autonomie sowie ihre traditionellen berufliche Kultur beibehalten können.[75] Die Autoren erwähnen unter anderem die Rolle des „clinical manager", d.h. ein Arzt, welcher eine Management-

---

70 Festa/Walmsley (2005).
71 Dubs (2005), S. 169.
72 Hollmann (2010), S. 2 f.
73 Hollmann (2010), S. 3.
74 Dubs (2005).
75 Byrkjeflot/Jespersen (2014), S. 18.

Funktion im Spital übernimmt, ohne seine medizinische Tätigkeit komplett aufzugeben. Dank seinem Einblick in beide Welten wird einem solchen „hybrid manager" die wichtige Funktion zugesprochen, zwischen der professionellen Logik der Selbstorganisation und der neuen Management-Logik vermitteln und übersetzen zu können.[76] Es liegt nahe sich hier zu überlegen, ob diese Idee des „hybrid managers" auch auf Richter in Führungspositionen übertragbar ist.

2.4 Führung von Richtern

Das Führen im Gericht hatte lange Zeit einen niedrigen Stellen- 170
wert und beschränkte sich bei den vorsitzenden Richtern meist aufs reine Verwalten.[77] Spätestens seit der NPM Reform, wo unter anderem auch das Prinzip der Führungsorientierung in den Vordergrund gerückt ist, wird von vielen Autoren anerkannt, dass ein Gericht als grosser Dienstleistungsbetrieb mit einer möglichst professionellen Administration auch auf eine ebenso effiziente Führung angewiesen ist.[78] Trotz einem breiten Forschungsinteresse zu Leadership und dessen Einfluss und Faktoren stellt Wice einen Mangel an empirischer Forschung über Leadership im Justizbereich fest. So existiere keine generelle Analyse, wie Richter die Führung in dieser komplexen bürokratischen Organisation bewältigen.[79] Insbesondere wird die spezifische Führung von Richtern in der Literatur nicht oder nur sehr wenig behandelt. Klopfer[80] betont zudem, dass der Begriff der Führung im Gericht vor allem in den Rechtsprechungseinheiten Widerstand und Verunsicherung auslöst.

Im Folgenden soll die Literatur zur direkten Personalführung von 171
Richtern zusammengefasst werden. In Anlehnung an die bereits erwähnten Definition der direkten Personalführung von Kolb[81] beinhaltet dies die Fragen danach, **wer** die Richter führt oder führen soll, **was** (welcher Aufgabenbereich) konkret geführt werden kann und soll, **wie** (mit welchen Führungsinstrumenten) geführt wird und **wozu** (welche Zielerreichung) Richter geführt werden sollen.

---

76 BYRKJEFLOT/JESPERSEN (2014), S. 8.
77 KLOPFER (2007).
78 WIPFLI (2006).
79 WICE (1995).
80 KLOPFER (2007).
81 KOLB (2008).

Wer kann Richter führen?

172 Im Bereich der justizinternen Führung existieren verschiedene Führungsmodelle. Die direkte Personalführung übt in der Regel die Leitung des Gerichts aus (in der Schweiz: Gerichtspräsident, Verwaltungskommission, Geschäftsleitung), welche die Gesamtverantwortung für die Justizverwaltung trägt. Einen Teil der Führungsverantwortung tragen auch die Kammer- oder Abteilungspräsidenten, welche die finanzielle und personelle Organisation sowie die Einheit und Koordination der Rechtsprechung in ihrem Bereich sicherstellen sollen. Diese werden im administrativen Bereich richterlicher Führungsfunktionen üblicherweise unterstützt von Generalsekretären, Justizmanagern oder leitenden Gerichtsschreibern.[82] Gemäss der Studie von Cameron, Zimmermann und Downling[83] kann es dabei zu Schwierigkeiten bei der Klärung der Hierarchie und Zuständigkeiten zwischen Verwaltungsverantwortlichen und Richtern in Führungspositionen kommen. Besonders die Beziehung von Gerichtsverwaltung und -Präsident sei aufgrund verschiedener Kulturen und Werten häufig von Konflikten geprägt sowie durch ein gewisses Misstrauen der Richter gegenüber „Non-professionals".[84] Auch tun sich Gerichtspräsidenten oftmals schwer damit, administrative Aufgaben zu delegieren, da sie die Kontrolle, und im breiteren Sinne ihre Macht, nicht verlieren wollen. Gemäss Cameron und Zimmermann kann diese unklare Rollenfunktion so geklärt werden, dass der Gerichtspräsident die Aufgabe der Verwaltungsführung auf der Mikroebene wahrnimmt, also die Führung im direkten Umgang mit den Mitarbeitern, während die Gerichtsverwaltung den Überblick über die Verwaltung haben sollte.[85] In der Literatur findet man jedoch nichts Genaueres über die direkte Führungsverantwortung über die Richter selbst.

173 Zentral ist hier die Frage nach der Akzeptanz der Richter gegenüber einer Führungsperson und ihren Entscheidungen. Gemäss Klopfer ist diese nur dann gegeben, wenn es sich bei der führenden Person ebenfalls um eine Richterperson mit den jeweiligen Kenntnissen des Gerichtswesens handelt.[86] Eine Schwierigkeit in diesem Zusammenhang ist, dass die Führungskompetenzen im Rahmen von Wahlen von Richtern in Führungspo-

---

82 POLTIER (2012), LIENHARD (2009).
83 CAMERON/ZIMMERMANN/DOWLING (1987).
84 CAMERON et al. (1987).
85 CAMERON et al. (1987).
86 KLOPFER (2007).

sitionen nicht oder nicht genügend in Betracht gezogen werden. Oftmals wird bei der Auswahl des Gerichtspräsidenten aufgrund politischer Gründe entschieden oder nach dem Anciennitätsprinzip verfahren. Theoretisch ist man sich einig, dass nur noch solche Richter in ein Führungsamt gewählt werden sollten, welche sich ihrer Führungsaufgabe bewusst sind und diese auch erfüllen können. In der Praxis wird dies aber längst nicht immer umgesetzt.[87]

Zwar scheint derjenige Richter, welcher die Funktion des Gerichts- 174
oder Abteilungspräsidenten innehat über eine gewisse Zusatzfunktion im Bereich der Personalführung zu verfügen. Eine solche Führungsverantwortung ist jedoch ständig mit den Begriffen des „Primus inter pares" und der „richterlichen Unabhängigkeit" konfrontiert. Die richterliche Unabhängigkeit hat zum Ziel, unzulässige und sachfremde Einmischungen oder Einflüsse in die richterliche Entscheidungsfindung zu verhindern. Der Richter ist bei der Ausübung der Rechtsprechung alleine dem Gesetz unterworfen.[88] Die richterliche Unabhängigkeit beinhaltet neben der institutionellen Unabhängigkeit gegenüber dem externen Einfluss anderer (Staats-)Gewalten auch die im Zusammenhang mit der Personalführung wichtige personenbezogenen Unabhängigkeit.[89] Dies hat zur Konsequenz, dass sich der unabhängige Richter im Gegenteil zu anderen Mitarbeitern in der Ausübung seiner Rechtsprechungsfunktion nicht in einem Unterordnungsverhältnis zur Führung befindet.[90] Der Präsident des Gerichts ist dabei in der Rolle des „Primus inter pares", also der Erste unter Gleichrangigen. Es handelt sich hier um einen Widerspruch in sich, da es besagt, dass alle im gleichen Rang stehen aber eben doch einer eine Vorzugsstellung besitzt.[91] Mosimann[92] spricht bei dieser besonderen Situation von einer internen, „*sozusagen funktionalen*" Hierarchie ohne formelle Führungskompetenz, also einer Art informeller und kollegialer Führung.

Die personenbezogene richterliche Unabhängigkeit bedingt neben der 175
Weisungsungebundenheit in der Rechtsprechung gleichzeitig auch die Selbständigkeit des Richters im Spruchkörper.[93] Im Rahmen der richterli-

---

87 KLOPFER (2007), WIPFLI (2006).
88 VALOIS (2012), S. 374 ff.
89 KIENER (2001), S. 13.
90 KLOPFER (2007).
91 CAVELTI (2013), S. 112.
92 MOSIMANN (2013), S. 12.
93 KIENER (2001), S. 221 ff.

chen Entscheidungsfindung muss somit die Teilnahme und Gleichwertigkeit der Stimme jedes Richters gelten. Während die Führung der nichtrichterlichen Justizarbeiter oftmals durch eine autoritäre Führung mit Weisungskompetenzen der Führungskraft geprägt ist, kommt im Richterkollegium ein basisdemokratischer Entscheidungsfindungsprozess zum Einsatz.[94] Dies schliesst grundsätzlich aus, dass der Vorsitzende des Gerichts mit Stichentscheid beeinflussen kann.[95] Kiener ist sogar der Meinung, dass Richter in Führungsfunktionen regelmässig und turnusgemäss wechseln sollten, damit einer möglichen Machtverfestigung und einem Ungleichgewicht entgegengewirkt und die materielle Gleichwertigkeit der Stimmkraft garantiert werden kann. Eine gewisse, wenn auch kaum fassbare Hierarchisierung kann sich dabei höchstens aus persönlichen Eigenschaften der Richter wie Lebensalter, Anciennität und persönlicher Autorität ergeben.[96]

176 Die schwierige Situation lässt sich am Beispiel der Frage verdeutlichen, wer dazu berechtigt wäre, Leistungsbeurteilungen als typisches Personalförderungs- und Entwicklungsinstrument durchzuführen. Dies in Verbindung mit der ebenfalls berechtigten Frage, ob Leistungserwartungen an den einzelnen Richter überhaupt legitim sind. Der Generalsekretär des Bundesgerichts vertrat dazu die Meinung, dass es durchaus die Aufgabe der Gerichtsleitung sein könnte, die von einer höheren Aufsichtsbehörde definierten Zielvorgaben zum Geschäftsgang (wie bspw. Fallzahlen pro Einheit) an die Abteilungen und Kammern weiterzugeben und minimale Einzelziele für Richter zu definieren.[97] Doch ist der führende Richter befugt, seine Richterkollegen nach solchen Leistungszielen zu beurteilen oder muss dies immer durch eine obere Instanz geschehen? Laut Mosimann fehlt den Richterkollegen in Führungspositionen für richterliche Leistungsbeurteilungen die nötige Legitimität, Akzeptanz sowie auch Kompetenz.[98] Es bleibt unklar, ob die beurteilenden Instanzen, d.h. der Gerichtspräsident, der Abteilungspräsident oder ein anderes innergerichtliches Aufsichtsorgan, zur Ausübung einer solchen Aufgabe einerseits kompetent und andererseits legitimiert wären. Hier zu erwähnen ist die Situation im Kanton Bern, wo die für eine Gerichtseinheit verantwortliche

94 Cameron et al. (1987).
95 Cavelti (2013). S. 327.
96 Kiener (2001), S. 339.
97 Tschümperlin (2009), S. 235.
98 Mosimann (2013), S. 12.

Person mit den betreffenden Richtern pro Jahr ein Standortgespräch durchführt. Dabei sind einerseits die allgemeine Situation (wie Rahmenbedingungen und Geschäftslast) sowie Fach- und Verhaltenskompetenzen ein Thema und andererseits kann auch über Führungsverantwortung gesprochen werden.[99] Eine alternative Möglichkeit ist die Selbstbeurteilung des Richters, wie sie in der Idee des Richterportfolios in Zürich[100] umgesetzt ist.[101] Dabei wird bewusst auf eine externe Evaluierung der erbrachten Leistung oder eine Supervision verzichtet.

Disziplinarischen Aspekte der Führung werden durch die formelle Dienstaufsicht im Rahmen der Justizaufsicht der Richter abgedeckt. Persönliche Verhaltensweisen eines Richters können dann Gegenstand eines Disziplinarverfahrens werden, wenn strafbares Verhalten oder individuell vorwerfbare Verstösse gegen Amtspflichten vorliegen.[102] Sanktionen in Form von Verweisen, Bussen oder sogar einer Abberufung werden nur durch grob fehlerhaftes Verhalten gerechtfertigt. Dazu gehören konkret Vorgänge, welche die richterlichen Verhaltenspflichten gegenüber den Parteien verletzen oder sonst in ernsthafter und objektiver Weise Ansehen und Unabhängigkeit des Amtes beeinträchtigen, wie bspw. ungebührliche Äusserungen gegenüber Parteien oder die bewusste Verschleppung von Verfahren.[103] Die Dienstaufsicht erlaubt es in erster Linie, die Verfahrensfairness sicherzustellen und gemäss Mahon und Schaller[104] mögliche „*erreurs de casting*", also das Rekrutieren von inkompetenten und nicht geeigneten Richtern, zu korrigieren. Ausgeübt wird die rechtlich streng geregelte Disziplinaraufsicht aufgrund des enormen Druckpotentials auf die richterliche Unabhängigkeit durch eine unabhängige Behörde.[105] Je nach gerichtsinterner Kompetenzordnung oder gesetzlicher Kompetenzzuweisung handelt es sich dabei um ein übergeordnetes Justizorgan, eine rich- 177

---

99 GRÜTTER (2012).

100 Ziel des 2004 entwickelten und ab 2007 definitiv in Zürich eingeführten Richterportfolios ist es, den Richtern eine flexible, selbstorganisierte und bedarfsgerechte Fortbildung und Entwicklung in allen Kompetenzen der richterlichen Tätigkeiten zu bieten. Oberste Bedingung ist, dass die richterliche Unabhängigkeit nicht gefährdet wird (LICHTI ASCHWANDEN, 2010).

101 LICHTI ASCHWANDEN (2010).

102 KIENER (2001), S. 304.

103 KIENER (2001), S. 305 f.

104 MAHON/SCHALLER (2013), S. 10 f.

105 KIENER (2001), S. 305.

terliche Kommission oder ein neutrales Gericht.[106] Während es in Deutschland Standard ist, dass eine gerichtsinterne Dienstaufsicht durch die jeweilige Präsidentschaft des Gerichts besteht, kennt die Schweizer so gut wie keine derart formalisierte gerichtsinterne und verfahrensmässig abgesicherte Leistungskontrolle.[107]

Welche Aufgabenbereiche sollen geführt werden?

178 Konkret hat die direkte Personalführung gemäss Thom und Ritz[108] zur Aufgabe, die zentralen Personalprozesse, d.h. die Personalgewinnung, -Beurteilung, -Einsatz und -Erhaltung sowie die Personalentwicklung und -Freistellung umzusetzen und insbesondere die Aktivierung der Mitarbeitermotivation und Leistungsbereitschaft sicherzustellen. Im Rahmen der Führung von Richtern muss beachtet werden, dass die Personalgewinnung sowie die -Freistellung in den meisten Fällen nicht im Aufgabenbereich des Justizmanagements liegen, sondern in der Schweiz einer politischen Wahl durch das Parlament oder vereinzelt durch das Volk unterstellt ist.[109]

179 Eine entscheidende Frage bei den restlichen Führungsaufgaben ist, wie weit die richterliche Unabhängigkeit vor Weisungen des Vorsitzenden schützt. Dies leitet auf die zweite Frage über, bei welchen Aufgaben die Richter durch einen Vorsitzenden geführt werden können. Oder umgekehrt gefragt: Wann sind Richter befugt, sich der Führung des Gerichtspräsidenten mit dem Bezug auf ihre Unabhängigkeit zu entziehen? Die persönliche Unabhängigkeit des Richters rechtfertigt nicht jedes Verhalten, wie bspw. das Widersetzen gegenüber einer Einteilung in bestimmte Abteilungen, Nichteinhaltung der Präsenzpflicht, die Verweigerung einer sinnvollen Zusammenarbeit oder die Nichteinhaltung von Zitierregeln.[110] Genauso wie die gesamte Justiz[111] untersteht auch der einzelne Richter dem Leistungsprinzip, d.h. er ist zur Effizienz und Effektivität bei der Erledigung seiner Arbeit verpflichtet. In der Literatur wird unterschieden zwischen der richterlichen Unabhängigkeit in der Rechtsprechungsfunktion und in der administrativen Führung, welche eine effiziente Justizverwaltung sicherstellt.

---

106 TANQUEREL (2014), S. 22.
107 RASELLI (2011).
108 THOM/RITZ (2013).
109 MOSIMANN (2013), S. 2.
110 MOSIMANN (2013), S. 6.
111 *«Dans l'ensemble, la justice doit (...) être efficace»* (POLTIER, 2011, S. 1018).

Die richterliche Unabhängigkeit kann sich nur auf die richterliche Tätigkeit der Rechtsprechung („activité juridictionnelle") beziehen, nicht aber auf Fragen der Führung und Funktionsweise des Gerichts. Der Richter unterscheidet sich nur insofern von anderen Berufskategorien, als er aufgrund der richterlichen Unabhängigkeit im Rahmen seiner Rechtsprechung keinem Aufsichtsregime unterworfen sein darf.[112] Weisungsbefugnisse des vorsitzenden Richters sind dementsprechend nur in den Bereichen ausgeschlossen, wo die richterliche Unabhängigkeit des Richters bedroht ist. Reine Verwaltungsanordnungen und organisatorische Vorgaben beschränken die richterliche Unabhängigkeit in der Regel nicht. Führung auch mit Weisungsbefugnissen sei dort berechtigt und sogar dringend notwendig, wo es zur effizienten und effektiven Selbstverwaltung der Justiz beiträgt.[113] Damit liege es im Interesse einer effizienten Justizverwaltung, dass führende Richter auch Weisungen über organisatorische Vorgaben, Führungsindikatoren und administrativen Verfahrensgänge festlegen können. In diesem Sinne meint Kiener,[114] dass eine doppelte Stimmkraft eines vorsitzenden Richters im Bereich der Justizverwaltung gerechtfertigt sei. Eine gewisse zwingende Einflussnahme sollte gemäss Cavelti[115] auch für Abteilungspräsidenten möglich sein, ohne jedes Mal die Zustimmung der Gesamtführung des Gerichts (Gerichtspräsidium) zu erhalten, wo die individuelle Einflussnahme aufgrund der mehrköpfigen Besetzung ohnehin beschränkt ist. Im Bereich der administrativen Aufgaben erwähnt Cavelti konkret die Kompetenz der Führung, die Richter zu verpflichten, formale Eingangsbestätigungen innerhalb einer Frist zu verschicken oder die telefonische Erreichbarkeit sicherzustellen sowie Bestimmungen über die schriftliche Ausführung der Urteile zu erlassen. 180

Die Umsetzung eines konsequenten Justizmanagements ist gemäss Wipfli[116] mit einer teilweisen Abkehr vom „Primus inter pares" Gedanken im Bereich administrativer Führungsprozesse verbunden. Die Führungsorientierung als wichtiges Element eines modernen Justizsmanagements kann nur mit einem starken Präsidium umgesetzt werden. Klar ist, dass sich die hierarchische Unterordnungsbeziehung sofort dann aufheben muss, wenn es sich um Fragen und Tätigkeiten im Bereich der Rechtspre- 181

[112] TANQUEREL (2014), S. 17.
[113] CAVELTI (2013), S. 332.
[114] KIENER (2001), S. 339.
[115] CAVELTI (2013), S. 330.
[116] WIPFLI (2006).

chung handelt. Jeglicher Druck auf die Richtung der Rechtsprechung ist nicht mit der richterlichen Unabhängigkeit vereinbar[117]. Tanquerel[118] betont mehrmals, dass der Bereich der Führung im Gericht ein unbestimmter Begriff ist, der je nach Interpretation mehr oder weniger beinhaltet. Eine Abgrenzung zwischen dem administrativen und dem richterlichen Tätigkeitsbereich scheint in Theorie und Praxis oft schwierig zu sein, da einerseits die Grenze nicht immer klar ist und es andererseits auch eine Überschneidung der beiden Zonen gibt, wo diese miteinander interagieren. Gemäss Martens[119] kann die interne Unabhängigkeit nicht nur durch Beeinflussung im Rahmen der Urteilsfindung, sondern eben auch durch zu hierarchische Richtlinien, Evaluationen, Forderungen nach mehr Kohärenz und Anreize zu schnellen und konformen Urteilen gefährdet werden. Auch Poltier[120] weist darauf hin, dass rein organisatorische oder administrative Vorschriften und Vorgaben durchaus geeignet sind, einen gewissen Druck auf die Rechtsprechung auszuüben. Auf der anderen Seite können Störungen in der Funktionsweise des Gerichts, wie bspw. die Überbelastung der Gerichte, überdurchschnittlich hohe Abwesenheitsquoten, ineffiziente Arbeitsweise, interne Konflikte oder unangepasste Verhaltensweisen der Richter ausserhalb der richterlichen Urteilsfindung auch die Qualität der Rechtsprechung und somit der gesamten Justiz negativ beeinflussen[121]. Dass es sich hierbei um eine ungeklärte Abgrenzung handelt, zeigt sich insbesondere bei der Diskussion über die Vereinbarkeit von Führungsinstrumenten mit der richterlichen Unabhängigkeit. Ein Beispiel dafür ist die im nächsten Abschnitt thematisierte Diskussion um richterliche Leistungsbeurteilung.

Wie können Richter geführt werden?

182 Zu möglichen internen Führungsinstrumenten gehören in der Justiz u.a. Leistungs- und Verhaltensbeurteilungen, internes Controlling, Mitarbeitergespräche und Fort- und Weiterbildungen.[122] Wie bereits im vorherigen Abschnitt diskutiert, ist der Einsatz von Führungsinstrumenten grundsätzlich dann erlaubt, wenn sie die richterliche Unabhängigkeit nicht gefährden, also hauptsächlich administrative Ziele verfolgen. Wenn man

117 POLTIER (2012).
118 TANQUEREL (2014), S. 16, 19.
119 MARTENS (2013).
120 POLTIER (2011).
121 TANQUEREL (2014), S. 24.
122 WIPFLI (2006).

die Literatur dazu durchforscht, entdeckt man jedoch Uneinigkeiten bei der Frage, welche Art und Ausgestaltung von Führungsinstrumenten im Bereich der Führung von Richtern legitim sind und welche nicht. Im Allgemeinen findet man wenige Hinweise auf die konkrete Umsetzung von Führungsinstrumenten. Dies könnte mit dem im vorherigen Abschnitt erwähnten Problem zusammenhängen, dass die Abgrenzung zwischen dem richterlichen und administrativen Führungsbereich aufgrund Überschneidungen nicht immer klar zu definieren ist und damit immer die Diskussion um die Vereinbarkeit mit der richterlichen Unabhängigkeit im Zentrum steht.

Ein Beispiel, welches diese Unsicherheit veranschaulicht, ist die äus- 183
serst aktuelle, aber noch eher wenig erforschte Diskussion zu richterliche Leistungsvorgaben und -beurteilungen (siehe auch Lienhard, 2014). Führung bedingt, dass Informationen und Methoden zur Verfügung stehen, anhand welcher die Arbeit an den Gerichten und dementsprechend auch die richterliche Arbeit erfasst werden kann. Gemäss Mosimann sind qualitative und quantitative Ansprüche an die richterliche Tätigkeit durchaus gerechtfertigt, da auch Vorstellungen darüber existieren, was den Ansprüchen nicht genügt. Qualitätssicherung ist ein grundsätzlich berechtigter Ansatz, da Genügen oder Ungenügen im Amt keine Frage von Unabhängigkeit ist[123]. In dem Sinne urteilt Lienhard (2014), dass eine wirksame Qualitätskontrolle sowie die richterliche Leistungsbeurteilung aus justizverfassungsrechtlicher Sicht zulässig und sogar notwendig sind. Die entscheidende Frage dreht sich demnach nicht um die Legitimität der Qualitätskontrolle von richterlicher Arbeit an sich, sondern um die Frage nach geeigneten Mitteln und Indikatoren.[124]

Gemäss Kettiger[125] scheint in der Schweiz die Leistungserfassung als 184
internes Führungsinstrument von Richtern zugelassen zu sein. Dies jedoch nur im Rahmen von Controlling als Ist-Werte und nicht im Sinne verbindlicher Leistungsvorgaben. Weiter wird die Art der Verwendung solcher Informationen diskutiert. Sind Leistungsbeurteilungen nur dann legitim, solange sie ausschliesslich zum internen Gebrauch bestimmt sind und als sog. Personalförderungs- und Entwicklungsinstrumente im Sinne einer Selbstbeurteilung eingesetzt werden[126] oder ist gar ein externer Gebrauch

[123] MOSIMANN (2011).
[124] KETTIGER, 2003.
[125] KETTIGER, 2003.
[126] WIPFLI (2006).

solcher Daten gerechtfertigt? So sind im Rahmen des Controllingkonzepts des Bundesgerichts gewisse richterspezifische Informationen nicht vollständig der Oberaufsicht bzw. (Wieder-)Wahlbehörde zugänglich.[127] Als problematisch für die richterliche Unabhängigkeit wird insbesondere die Veröffentlichung solcher Leistungsindikatoren und der damit einhergehende Rechtfertigungsdruck gegenüber der Öffentlichkeit und den Prozessparteien gewertet. Mosimann kommt zum Schluss, dass eine formelle Leistungsbeurteilung nicht möglich ist, da sich richterliche Qualitäten kaum in formale und rechtsgleich anwendbare Raster übertragen lassen. Daher beurteilt er diese auch als Instrument der Laufbahn-Lenkung als ungeeignet.[128] Cavelti[129] empfindet den totalen Widerstand gegen individuelle Wirkungs- und Leistungsvorgaben für einzelne Richter als zu absolut. Unmöglich in der Schweiz, da sie als unvereinbar mit der richterlichen Unabhängigkeit gelten, sind individuelle positive oder negative Leistungsanreize wie Leistungslohn oder Lohnkürzungen.[130]

185 Ähnliche Fragen stellen sich bei der Zuteilung der Arbeitslast. Muss deren Objektivität stets mittels rein formaler Kriterien gewährleistet werden oder sind allenfalls auch Zuteilungen durch die führende Justizperson möglich, bei denen die Spezialkenntnisse und Kapazität der jeweiligen Richter miteinbezogen werden? Die Befürchtungen bei einer nicht rein auf formalen Kriterien beruhenden Fallzuteilung sind, dass dabei auf Vorlieben oder sogar Einstellungen einzelner Richter Rücksicht genommen und dadurch das Urteil im Voraus unzulässig beeinflusst wird.[131]

Wozu sollen Richter geführt werden?

186 Bei der Beschäftigung mit der direkten Führung von Richtern wird klar, dass diese in einem permanenten Spannungsverhältnis mit gewichtigen rechtlichen und berufsspezifischen Prinzipien steht. Gerade weil über die Tragweite dieser Prinzipien nicht immer Einigkeit herrscht, können sie die Vorstellung über Leadership entscheidend prägen und müssen bei der Frage nach einer möglichen richterlichen Führung unbedingt in Betracht gezogen werden. Trotz dieser Kontroverse seien Führungsstrukturen, insbesondere auch formeller Art, laut Kettiger[132] zur Sicherstellung einer

---

[127] LIENHARD/KETTIGER (2011).
[128] MOSIMANN (2013), S. 13.
[129] CAVELTI (2013).
[130] CAVELTI (2013), S. 330, MOSIMANN (2013), S. 12.
[131] CAVELTI (2013), S. 331.
[132] KETTIGER (2003).

effizienten und effektiven Rechtspflege sowie der rechts- und ordnungsgemässen Verwendung staatlicher Mittel zwingend notwendig. Dies sei gerade hinsichtlich der steigenden Erwartungen an die Justiz von Seiten der externen Stakeholder von grosser Bedeutung. Das Gleiche gilt auch für die richterliche Arbeit, welche einen hohen Erwartungsdruck und damit einhergehend eine zunehmende Arbeitsbelastung im Richterberuf[133] auslösen können.[134] Eine erfolgreiche Personalführung kann einen positiven Einfluss haben auf die Leistungsmotivation, Zufriedenheit, Entwicklung und das organisationale Engagement der Richter. Dies wirkt sich wiederum positiv auf die Leistung und Zielerreichung der gesamten Justiz aus.[135] Die Studie von Wice[136] kommt überdies zum Schluss, dass das Vorhandensein effektiver, lokaler Führungsprozesse einen zentralen Faktor für den Erfolg einer Justizreform darstellt. Eine Reform ohne effektives Leadership ist auch mit genügend Ressourcen und machbaren Konzept kaum möglich. Gerade in der Justiz, welche sich traditionell als eher reformresistent zeigt, sei der Fokus auf die Führung deshalb besonders wichtig.

Für eine sachgerechte und wirksame Führung von Richtern braucht es 187
einerseits geeignete Führungsinstrumente. Bei der Justiz handelt es sich, wie es Poltier[137] formuliert, um eine *„entreprise très particulière“*, bei welcher die Qualität der Rechtsprechung und damit die Gewährung ihrer Unabhängigkeit stets an erster Stelle stehen muss. Nur weil im Bereich des Personalmanagements etwas „à la mode“ ist, heisst das noch lange nicht, dass dies auch sinnvoll sei für die Justiz.[138] Zusätzlich braucht es führende Richter mit dem Willen und den Fähigkeiten zur Übernahme von Führungsverantwortung und die Bereitschaft und Akzeptanz der Richter, administrative Anordnungen nicht gleich als Eingriff in die personenbezogene richterliche Unabhängigkeit zu qualifizieren.

---

[133] Ein Beispiel für eine spezifische Berufsbelastung des Richterberufs stellt gemäss der richterlichen Befragung von LUDEWIG (2008, S. 30f.) der Konflikt zwischen Arbeitsökonomie, d.h. dem Wunsch nach mehr Effizienz, und der Berufsethik bezüglich der Qualität der Rechtsprechung dar.

[134] LUDEWIG (2008).

[135] THOM/RITZ (2000).

[136] WICE (1995).

[137] POLTIER (2011), S. 1009.

[138] MOSIMANN (2013), S. 11.

2.5 Fazit der Literatur

188 Die direkte Personalführung ist gemäss der Leadership-Forschung entscheidend für die Aktivierung der Mitarbeitermotivation und –Entwicklung, der individuellen Leistungsbereitschaft und des Engagements zur Erreichung der organisationalen Ziele.[139] Zu der hier untersuchten Forschungsfrage nach der Bedeutung und Ausgestaltung der direkten Personalführung von Richtern besteht in der Literatur wie auch in der Praxis weitgehend Uneinigkeit. In Anlehnung an den kontextabhängigen Leadership-Ansatz muss dabei auf jeden Fall den Eigenheiten des Umfeldes der Justiz und der Richter, d.h. der jeweiligen Situation, dem Aufgabenbereich sowie den persönlichen Eigenschaften, Werten und Kultur Rechnung getragen werden.

189 Im spezifischen Kontext der Justiz lässt sich insbesondere auf die Eigenschaften einer professionellen Bürokratie von Mintzberg[140] verweisen. Es ist davon auszugehen, dass die Richter als Kernakteure der Justiz mit ihrer dominanten beruflichen Kultur die Möglichkeiten und Grenzen der direkten Personalführung entscheidend beeinflussen.[141] Die Berufskultur der Richter scheint besonders geprägt von der richterlichen Unabhängigkeit, weshalb die Richter über einen grossen Handlungsspielraum verfügen und dem Prinzip des „Primus inter pares", welche eine einseitige und hierarchisierte Führung unter Richtern trotz Führungsverantwortung des Gerichtspräsidenten auszuschliessen scheinen. Die auf Unabhängigkeit und basisdemokratische Entscheidungsprozesse hin ausgerichtete Berufskultur ist kaum vereinbar mit traditionellen Konzepten der transaktionalen Führung, welche auf Kontrollinstrumenten und zwingenden Führungsanweisungen basiert. Einen grösseren Mehrwert könnten hingegen der transformationale und instrumentelle Führungsansatz bereithalten, wo die Kommunikation einer gemeinsamen Vision und Ziele und das konstruktive Feedback im Vordergrund stehen. Diese moderneren Ansätze haben insbesondere die Mitarbeiterentwicklung, die Unterstützung der Mitarbeiter bei der Erfüllung ihrer Leistungsziele sowie die Vereinbarkeit ihrer Werte mit derjenigen der Organisation zum Ziel. Wenn man jedoch davon ausgeht, dass das Führungsverständnis der Richter wenig ausgeprägt ist und daher direkte Führung im Allgemeinen mit hierarchischen und direk-

---

139 VAN WART (2003).
140 MINTZBERG (1989).
141 BOUCKAERT (2007).

tiven Weisungen gleichgesetzt wird, könnte dies in einer allgemeine Abwehrhaltung gegenüber jeder Art von Führungskultur zum Ausdruck kommen.

In der Literatur wird von mehreren Seiten eine stärkere und formellere Führung im administrativen Bereich gefordert, welche die effektive und effiziente Selbstverwaltung der Justiz unterstützt und sicherstellt.[142] Eine effektive Personalführung sei zudem besonders wichtig für die erfolgreiche Umsetzung von Reformen.[143] Zur Abgrenzung zwischen richterlichen und administrativen Führungsprozessen und der dabei geltenden Tragweite der richterlichen Unabhängigkeit besteht allerdings Uneinigkeit. Gerade bei der Einführung neuer Führungsinstrumente und -Kompetenzen ist mit einer Abwehr von Seiten der Richter zu rechnen, welche ihren bisherigen Handlungsspielraum verteidigen wollen. Die Stellung des Gerichtspräsidenten als „Primus inter pares" könnte zusätzlich in einer Unsicherheit bei der Wahrnehmung seiner Führungsverantwortung resultieren. Aufgrund des einseitigen Fokus der Richter auf juristische Kompetenzen und Ressourcen scheint wahrscheinlich, dass gerade Führungs- und Managementkompetenzen im Gerichtsalltag eher vernachlässigt werden. 190

Da die Vereinbarkeit zwischen den Motivstrukturen und Werten der Organisation sowie denjenigen der einzelnen Mitarbeiter gemäss Thom und Ritz[144] am Anfang der Suche nach geeigneten Konzepten der Personalführung stehen soll, versucht die folgende Studie einen Einblick in die Realität der richterlichen Führung auf Basis der Wahrnehmungen und Vorstellungen der involvierten Justizakteure zu gewähren. 191

---

142 KETTIGER (2003), CAVELTI (2013).
143 WICE (1995).
144 THOM/RITZ (2000), S. 334.

3. Methode

192 Die vorliegende Arbeit ist Teil eines nationalen Forschungsprojekts zu Justizmanagement, welches vertieft die kulturelle Aufnahmefähigkeit der Schweizer Gerichte gegenüber Managementmethoden und -Instrumenten untersucht. Für diesen Artikel wurde eine Serie von halbstrukturierten Interviews (56) an Schweizerischen erst- sowie zweitinstanzlichen Gerichten durchgeführt und zwar sowohl an Zivil-, Straf- sowie Verwaltungsgerichten in neun Kantonen der drei schweizer Sprachregionen. Befragt wurden interne Justizakteure wie Richter, Gerichtsschreiber, Generalsekretäre und Justizmanager, sowie auch externe Akteure wie Politiker, Anwälte und Journalisten. Das Hauptziel dieser Gespräche war es, Erkenntnisse zu den verschiedenen Sichtweisen der Akteure über die aktuelle Funktionsweise der Gerichte und den Veränderungen der Organisation der Dritten Gewalt zu erfahren. Die Personen wurden angehalten, über ihre Vision der Justiz zu sprechen, die Qualitäten einer „guten Justiz" zu identifizieren sowie Bedrohungen und Chancen im Hinblick auf die Einführung von Managementmethoden in der Justiz zu nennen. Ein besonderer Fokus lag dabei auf der Definition der Rolle der Richter im Rahmen des Justizmanagements. Unter anderem wurden während den Interviews folgende Fragstellungen abgefragt:

- *Wie würden Sie die Entwicklungen und Veränderungen der letzten Jahre im Bereich der Führungsmethoden und der Organisation der Gerichte in Folge der Reformen der Dritten Gewalt beschreiben?*
- *Wer oder welche Instanz ist Ihrer Meinung nach verantwortlich für das Management im Gericht?*
- *Wie nehmen Sie das Justizmanagement im Allgemeinen wahr? Wird das Gericht gut oder schlecht geführt? Welches sind die Stärken im Bereich des Justizmanagements und welche Punkte könnten verbessert werden?*
- *Wie würden Sie die Akzeptanz der Richter gegenüber den Management-Methoden beurteilen (legislative und organisationale Reformen)? Haben Sie eine Entwicklung dieser Akzeptanz bemerkt in den letzten Jahren?*
- *Welches sind Ihrer Meinung nach die Qualitäten eines „guten Richters"?*
- *Welches sind Ihrer Meinung nach die Qualitäten eines „guten Managers"?*
- *Können Sie definieren, was für sie eine „gute Justiz" und ein „gutes Gericht" ausmacht?*

Die Interviews, welche jeweils etwa eine Stunde dauerten, wurden gemäss einer induktiven Methodologie[145] mit dem Ziel geführt, einen Gesamtüberblick der Hauptargumente der Befragten zu erhalten bis hin zu einer Ausschöpfung der Argumentation.[146] Die gespeicherten Aufnahmen der Interviews wurden daraufhin transkribiert und mithilfe der qualitativen Forschungssoftware NVivo 10™ kodiert, um die zentralen Antriebe und Hemmnisse („freins" und „facilitateurs") bei der Einführung des Management in der Justiz zu identifizieren. 193

Im Rahmen des hier vorliegenden Kapitels wurden die Argumente herausgefiltert und analysiert, welche sich zur Führung von Richtern finden liessen. Gerade bei Fragen zur Funktionsweise der Justiz im Allgemeinen, zur Komptabilität von Managementansätzen mit Eigenschaften der Justiz sowie zur Rolle des Richters wurden immer wieder relevante Aussagen über die Führung von Richtern gemacht. Für die Analyse wurden insbesondere die Aussagen in den Kodierungskategorien der *Hemmnisse* und *Antriebe* für das Management von Seiten der Richter ausgewertet. Angesichts der enormen Fülle an Daten (mehr als 1000 transkribierte Seiten) schien uns eine integrale Analyse der vorhandenen Daten nicht geeignet. Dies kann dementsprechend als Grenze unseres methodischen Ansatzes gesehen werden sowie auch die Stichprobe der interviewten Personen, welche nicht einer repräsentativen Methode entspricht. Dennoch ist es wichtig, sich daran zu erinnern, dass das Prinzip der qualitativen Ausschöpfung der Argumente gute Chancen hat, einen wesentlichen Teil der (wahrgenommene) Realität der Schweizer Justiz zu reflektieren und die sog. *qualitative Validität* sicherzustellen. 194

---

145 STRAUSS/CORBIN (2004).
146 MARTINEAU (2005).

4. Zusammenfassung der Aussagen der Befragten

195 Aus den im Rahmen dieser Studie geführten Gesprächen mit den verschiedenen Justizakteuren lassen sich zahlreiche interessante Aspekte dazu identifizieren, was Herausforderungen aber auch die Chancen einer direkten Führung von Richtern darstellen. Im Folgenden werden die Hauptaussagen zu den vier Definitionselementen der direkten Führung von Richtern (Wer? Was? Wie? Wozu?) präsentiert.

4.1 Wer ist legitimiert und akzeptiert für die Führung von Richtern?

196 Generell sind es Richter gewohnt, bei allen Fragen im Richter-Kollegium mitentscheiden zu dürfen. Es ist daher stets eine gewisse Abwehrhaltung bei der Zentralisierung von Entscheidungskompetenzen zu spüren. Als Grund dafür wird von Justizakteuren mit Führungsaufgaben die Angst der Richter genannt, an Macht und Kontrolle zu verlieren: *«Die Akzeptanz für eine Kompetenzverschiebung zuhanden der Präsidentin wäre bei den Richtern kaum vorhanden, weil sie es sich gewohnt sind, im Gremium mitentscheiden zu dürfen»; «Man hat Angst, man verliert als Richter an Entscheidungskompetenzen und vielleicht auch an Informationen»*. Die Wichtigkeit des Einbezugs der Richter in jede Entscheidungsfindung wird mehrmals betont: *«Gerade der Einbezug der Richterinnen und Richter ist enorm wichtig. Weil es ja die höchste Instanz ist, als eine Kollegialbehörde ist man einander gleich gestellt»; «Und deshalb führt das oft zu Misstrauen, wenn es Spitzen gibt in der Verwaltung, in welche die Richter nicht einbezogen sind»*.

197 Es scheint bei den Richtern ein Konsens darüber zu herrschen, dass eine richterliche Schulung eine notwendige Bedingung sei, um als glaubwürdige Führungskraft akzeptiert zu werden: *«Er muss sicher mal Richter gewesen sein. Es könnte schon ein Auswärtiger sein, aber er muss sicher mal Richter gewesen sein, sonst sagen die (die Richter) dann, dass er sich nicht in uns hinein versetzen kann»*. Oftmals wird von einer solchen Führung erwartet, dass sie zusätzlich über konkrete Erfahrungen und somit über weitreichende Kenntnisse der Gerichtsabläufe und den richterlichen Alltag verfügt: *«Richter, welche sich mit Führung beschäftigen, müssen immer noch eine richterliche Tätigkeit im Gericht ausführen, um ihre*

interne wie auch externe Glaubwürdigkeit zu wahren»[147] und *«Meiner Meinung nach ist es eine gute Sache, dass der Präsident/Staatsanwalt eine richterliche Tätigkeit behält, weil ein rein administrativ Verantwortlicher den Kern des Berufes nicht mehr kennen würde und schlechter geeignet wäre, gewisse Entscheidungen zu treffen».*[148] Dabei wird der Vergleich mit dem organisationalen Kontext des Spitals gezogen: *«Das geht auch im Spital nicht, wenn der Manager nichts von Medizin versteht».* Vielfach nicht akzeptiert als Führungspersonen werden Personen mit nicht-juristischer Ausbildung wie auch Gerichtsschreiber: *«Schlussendlich hat das einfach der leitende Gerichtsschreiber gemacht, aber der hatte auch nicht wirklich die Autorität, vor allem über die Richter nicht».* Doch selbst bei Erfüllung aller notwendigen Eigenschaften, wird die Legitimität einer Person, die Richter führt, dennoch angezweifelt: *«Er hätte mehr Legitimität (als Richter) aber man würde hintenherum schlecht reden und die Angst bliebe dieselbe».*[149]

Von nicht wenigen Justizakteuren wird aber gleichzeitig auch die 198
Wichtigkeit von Management-Kompetenzen genannt oder zumindest ein gewisses Interesse und/oder Begabung dafür. So empfindet es eine Generalsekretärin als schade, *«wenn man in Führungsfunktionen keine Menschen zulässt mit entsprechender Führungsausbildung und mit Führungserfahrung».* Auch ein Richter bestätigt: *«Das zentrale ist die Qualität der Richter, welche als administrative Chefs tätig sind, man muss Richter engagieren, die auch Manager sind»;*[150] *«(...) weil Primus inter pares sind die ersten Richter des Gerichts, aber in keinem Moment hat man ihre Management-Kompetenzen evaluiert».*[151] Jedoch gibt es insbesondere unter den Richtern auch Stimmen, die eine solche Management-

[147] *«Les juges qui s'occupent de la gestion doivent garder une activité juridictionnelle pour garder une crédibilité tant à l'interne qu'à l'externe (vis-à-vis du politique)».*

[148] *«A mon avis c'est une bonne chose que le président/procureur garde une activité juridictionnelle car un pur administrateur ne connaîtrait plus le cœur du métier et serait moins bon pour prendre certaine décision».*

[149] *«Il aura plus de légitimé mais on critiquerait par derrière et la crainte resterait la même».*

[150] *«Ce qui est primordial, c'est la qualité des magistrats qui vont fonctionner comme chefs administratifs, d'office, on doit engager des magistrats qui sont aussi des managers».*

[151] *«(...) parce que les Primus inter pares sont les premiers juges des tribunaux, mais à aucun moment que ce soit, on n'a évalué leurs compétences managériales».*

Ausbildung für unnötig halten: *«Ich stelle aber fest, dass das Kollegen in meinem Arbeitskreis nicht machen. Sie haben das Verständnis: Führen kann man von Amtes wegen. Und das finde ich problematisch»*. Diese Ansicht wird verdeutlicht durch die Aussage: *«Der Richter geht davon aus, dass er es nicht nötig hat im Bereich Management zu lernen, er praktiziert es und das reicht»*.[152] Oder sie würden sich gerne weiterbilden, finden es aber schwierig, einen geeigneten Kurs zu finden: *«Personalmanagement, ja klar, das sollte man machen. Diese Frage stellen wir uns auch. Ich habe aber noch keinen geeigneten Kurs gefunden. (...) Aber es ist noch schwierig, etwas zu finden, dass unseren Bedürfnissen entspricht»*.

199 Bei der Diskussion zur internen Funktionsweise des Gerichtsmanagements wird von unterschiedlichen Seiten angedeutet, dass Unklarheiten bei der Hierarchie der internen Organisation sowie in der Verteilung von administrativen Verantwortlichkeiten bestehen. So scheint oftmals nicht klar, an wen sich die Richter bei administrativen Fragen wenden sollen; an den administrativ Verantwortlichen (z.B. an den Generalsekretär oder leitenden Gerichtsschreiber) oder an den Gerichtspräsidenten. Das „Primus inter pares"-Prinzip wurde häufig von Richtern in Führungspositionen erwähnt, welche damit ihre Unsicherheit über ihre Rollen-Definition hinsichtlich des Verhältnisses zu den anderen Richtern ausdrückten. Ein Gerichtspräsident, welcher seine Führungsverantwortung ausüben möchte, sieht sich sogleich mit dem Gedanken konfrontiert, dass er *«ja eigentlich nicht der, der meinen Kollegen befehlen kann»* ist. *«Ich bin nur der Primus inter Pares»* und *«Es ist ziemlich kompliziert Leute zu führen, welche die gleiche Legitimität aufweisen wie du selbst, weil sie auch gewählt werden vom Grossrat, gibt es nicht wirklich eine Disziplinargewalt»*.[153]

4.2 Was kann und soll geführt werden?

200 Nicht bezweifelt ist, dass im juristischen Bereich die Unabhängigkeit des Richters eine klare Grenze für mögliche Weisungsbefugnisse einer Führungskraft darstellt. Was jedoch die Führung im administrativen

---

152 *«Le juge considère qu'il n'a pas besoin d'apprendre le management, il le pratique et c'est tout»*.

153 *«C'est assez compliqué de diriger des gens qui ont en fait la même légitimité que vous, parce qu'ils sont tous élus par le Grand conseil, il n'y a pas vraiment de pouvoir disciplinaire»*.

Bereich betrifft, gibt es Argumente in verschiedene Richtungen und die Grenzen werden unterschiedlich gesetzt. In den Interviews wurde häufig bemerkt, dass das Argument der richterlichen Unabhängigkeit von den Richtern auch eingesetzt wird, um sich jeglicher Art von Führung zu entziehen. Ein Gerichtspräsident, welcher neue administrative Instrumente einführen wollte, beschreibt seine missliche Ausgangslage mit der Aussage: *«Jeder achtet auf seine Unabhängigkeit. Und es gibt tatsächlich Leute, die glauben, ihre Unabhängigkeit sei schon gefährdet, wenn einer kommt und sagt, man müsse ein Kalendermodul bewirtschaften»*. In dieses Bild passt dann auch die Aussage eines Richters gegenüber seines Gerichtspräsidenten: *«Was erlauben Sie sich, sich in die Sache meiner Sekretärin einzumischen, das ist meine Angelegenheit».*[154] Das Argument der richterlichen Unabhängigkeit und damit die Verneinung der Legitimität einer direkten Führung wird in erster Linie bei sachbezogenen Führungsaufgaben aufgeworfen, welche die konkrete richterliche Arbeitsweise betreffen, wie bspw. bei administrativen Vorgaben zur Standardisierung von Arbeitsabläufen oder individuellen Leistungsbeurteilungen.

Bei der Frage, welche Aufgabenbereiche von einer richterlichen Füh- 201
rung erfasst werden sollten, werden von den Richtern in erster Linie personenbezogene Führungsaufgaben angesprochen. Diese betreffen in den meisten Fällen das Kommunizieren, Informieren und die Personalentwicklung. Einerseits wird das Bedürfnis nach mehr Feedback seitens der Führung genannt: *«Ein Standardgespräch einmal pro Jahr, so wie es Bern macht, wäre durchaus möglich. Aber das reich nicht, man muss vor allem auch zwischen durch, mehrmals pro Jahr mit den Leuten reden. Ich gehe davon aus, dass jede Abteilung nur dann funktioniert, wenn die Aufteilung der Arbeit durch den Abteilungsleiter funktioniert»*. Auch scheint die Kommunikation im Allgemeinen, insbesondere zwischen den Richtern selbst, ein grosses Thema zu sein, das im Gerichtsalltag nicht immer die gewünschte Aufmerksamkeit erhält. Eine zentrale Führungsaufgabe, die immer wieder angeschnitten wird, ist die Personalentwicklung: *«Ich finde, dass muss die Führung anpacken, dass die Leute, die es nötig haben, geschult werden»*. Während einige Justizakteure davon überzeugt sind, dass man Richter in gewissen Bereichen wie dem Management und der Führung gezielt weiterbilden sollte, sehen andere dies nicht als nötig an. Mehrfach erwähnt wird auch der Wunsch nach mehr Teamwork und bes-

[154] *«Comment vous permettez-vous de vous mêler des affaires de ma secrétaire, c'est mon affaire».*

serer Zusammenarbeit zwischen Richtern: *«Wenn man die Pflicht hätte, manchmal zusammen an einem Dossier zu arbeiten, wäre das besser. Aber die Richter mögen es nicht zu teilen. Man hat zu sehr die Gewohnheit, alleine zu arbeiten».*[155]

4.3 Wie ist die Führung von Richtern konkret umsetzbar?

202 Der Richter wird von den unterschiedlichsten Justizakteuren charakterisiert als *«einsames Tier, das es schlecht verträgt, wenn man ihm Befehle erteilt, auf allen Ebenen».*[156] Richter scheinen sich gegen jede Form von zwingendem Einfluss zu wehren: *«Für den Richter ist etwas Obligatorischen undenkbar».*[157] Sie wollen selbst entscheiden können, wie und wann sie ihre Arbeit erledigen: *«Es liegt in der Mentalität der Richter, sie sind sehr unabhängig in ihrer Arbeit und das ist sehr schwierig».*[158] So sind sie nicht bereit, sich dabei reinreden zu lassen: *«Sie sind es sich gewohnt, für sich in ihrer Ecke mit ihrem Gerichtsschreiber zu arbeiten und sie wollen das nicht ändern».*[159]

203 Dies bringt mit sich, dass unter den Richtern sehr unterschiedliche und individuell ausgeprägte Arbeitsmethoden angewendet werden. So erwähnt eine Gerichtsschreiberin: *«Wie man einen Fall anpackt, das ist unglaublich, das machen alle verschieden».* Daher wird die Idee einer minimalen Standardisierung der richterlichen Arbeitsmethode mithilfe gewisser administrativen Vorgaben gerade von Seiten der Gerichtsschreiber wie administrativ Verantwortlichen als wünschenswert erachtet: *«Ich finde es aber eigentlich schon bedauerlich, dass gerade bei einem kleinen Gericht wie bei uns, viele Dinge so unterschiedlich ablaufen. Das bekommen manchmal auch die Parteien mit. Ich würde es schon wünschenswert finden, wenn man sich ab und zu mehr absprechen würde, um einheitlicher zu werden, beispielsweise gerade bei der Struktur der Verhandlungsab-*

---

[155] *«Si on avait l'obligation de travailler parfois ensemble sur des dossiers ça serait mieux mais les juges n'aiment pas partager. On a trop l'habitude de travailler en solo maintenant ».*

[156] *«Étant un animal solitaire qui supporte mal qu'on lui donne des ordres, à tous les niveaux».*

[157] *«Pour le juge quelque chose d'obligatoire est impensable».*

[158] *«C'est dans la mentalité des juges, ils sont très indépendants dans leur travail, et c'est difficile».*

[159] *«Ils ont l'habitude de travailler dans leur coin avec leur greffier et ne veulent pas changer».*

läufe». Auf der anderen Seite stossen sie aber auch auf grossen Widerstand seitens der Richter. Viele sehen darin einen Schritt zur vollständigen Harmonisierung der Arbeitsmethoden und qualifizieren jede Standardisierung als Eingriff in die richterliche Unabhängigkeit.

Bei den zur Sprache gekommenen Führungsinstrumenten scheint das 204
Instrument der Leistungsbewertung und die Evaluation von richterlicher Arbeit ein wichtiges aber ungeklärtes Thema zu sein. Haupttenor bei den Richtern ist, dass richterliche Arbeit qualitativ schwer messbar ist und daher solche Qualitätsevaluationen nur begrenzt einsetzbar seien. Quantitative Messungen im Sinne von Anzahl Fälle pro Jahr/Semester seien ausserdem begrenzt aussagekräftig und teilweise *«willkürlich»*, da der Arbeitsaufwand für die einzelnen Fälle kaum vergleichbar sei. Ausserdem hätte eine solche Leistungskontrolle und -Vergleich *«sehr schlechte Auswirkungen auf das Arbeitsklima wie auch auf die Qualität der Rechtsprechung»*. Dennoch wird es von Gerichtspräsidenten nicht selten als Controlling-Instrument angewendet und teilweise sogar, wenn auch inoffiziell, als Benchmarking-Instrument zum Leistungsvergleich zwischen verschiedenen Richtern: *«Wenn man bei einem Richterpaar immer einen hat, der einfach doppelt so viele Pendenzen hat wie der andere, dann muss man sich schon fragen warum. Und wenn das jedes Jahr gleich ist, dann muss man sagen, du bist nicht so effizient wie der andere»*.

Auch bei Weiterbildungen als Instrument der Personalentwicklung gibt 205
es unterschiedliche Argumente. Einerseits werden sie von einigen Richtern als zwingend notwendig beurteilt, da sie kaum vorhanden sind im Gericht: *«Selbstkritisch muss ich aber sagen, dass das Führungsverständnis in der Justiz nicht sehr ausgeprägt ist und vor allem das Führungsvermögen nicht spezifisch geschult wird»*; *«Das ist ein fundamentaler Fehler, diese Weiterbildungen* (für Personen mit Führungsverantwortung im Gericht) *nicht als obligatorisch zu erklären».*[160] Andererseits ist aber auch die Vorstellung vorhanden, dass man gerade Kompetenzen im Bereich des Managements nicht erlernen kann oder muss und dass man Richter schon gar nicht dazu zwingen kann, solche Kurse zu besuchen: *«Ich denke, gerade die, die schon länger Richter sind, denken nicht, dass sie eine weitere Ausbildung brauchen»*.

---

160 *«C'est une erreur fondamentale de ne pas rendre ces formations obligatoires»*.

4.4 Wozu sollen Richter geführt werden?

206 Einerseits gibt es durchaus Justizakteure, welche die Überzeugung teilen, dass für eine effektive und effiziente Selbstverwaltung der Justiz nicht nur die Justiz an sich, sondern eben auch die Arbeit der Richter „*gut gemanagt*" werden muss. Dies kann wiederum nur mit einer geeigneten Führung, welche auch die Richter miteinbezieht, erreicht werden. Ein Gerichtspräsident umschreibt seine Erfahrungen wie folgt: «*Richter sind halt Häuptlinge und mit mehreren Häuptlingen wird's immer schwieriger. Und um diese Häuptlinge im Zaun zu halten, braucht's schon relativ eine straffe Führung*». Die Bedeutung von Führung ist gewissen Richtern also durchaus bewusst: «*Ob es gut läuft oder nicht, ist vor allem von der Leitungsfähigkeit der Abteilungsleiter abhängig. Eine Gefahr ist, dass die Politik Richter auswählt, die zwar gute Juristen sind, aber keine Leitungsfähigkeit haben*». Auch sehen einige Richter wie auch andere Justizakteure in einer gewissen Führung richterlicher Arbeitsmethoden eine Möglichkeit zur Steigerung der Effizienz und Transparenz der Arbeit der Justiz. Einen Schritt hin zur mehr Standards für die richterliche Arbeit deuten viele als Chance für mehr Einheitlichkeit und Koordination, was schlussendlich nicht nur für die richterliche Arbeit positiv ist (insbesondere fürs Zeitmanagement und den kollegialen Austausch), sondern auch in einer gerechteren Behandlung der übrigen Mitarbeitern sowie den Prozessparteien resultiert (z.B. durch einheitlichere und dadurch gerechtere Leistungsbeurteilung von Gerichtsschreibern oder der Verhandlungsführung): «*Es wäre einfacher, wenn es eine Führungsperson gibt, die auch die Richter führt. (...) Das wäre einfacher... und manchmal auch gerechter*». Als positives Outcome von Führung wird eine bessere Kommunikation und Feedbackkultur erwähnt, welche wiederum zu einer bessere Zusammenarbeit unter den Richtern sowie einer Stärkung der Selbstkritik führt. Eine Richterin meint dazu: «*Ich wollte das institutionalisieren, dass man nach jeder Verhandlung eine Feedbackrunde macht. Der Nutzen wäre eine bessere Zusammenarbeit der Kommission und auch für die Prozesspartei. Wenn ein gewisser Routineablauf besteht, dann gibt das auch eine Gleichbehandlung. Es läuft dann bei allen gleich ab*».

207 Weitaus häufiger herrscht unter den Richtern jedoch ein generelles Misstrauen gegenüber Managementmethoden, wozu auch jede Art von Führungskultur gehört. Managementansätze werden eher als intervenierende und im gewissen Sinne auch störende Kraft für die richterliche Arbeit wahrgenommen anstatt als Hilfsmittel. Oft wird die Befürchtung ge-

nannt, dass die Einführung neuer Management-Funktionen die Richter von ihrer Kernaufgabe (der Rechtsprechung) ablenken: «*Die Arbeit eines Richters ist es, Urteile zu fällen und nicht die Funktionsweise zu organisieren*».[161] Allgemein lässt sich zudem ein Desinteresse an der Funktionsweise des Gerichts feststellen: «*Der einfache Richter interessiert sich nicht für die administrative Funktionsweise seines Gerichts*».[162] Richter scheinen sich nicht für Fragen des Managements zu interessieren und sich auch nicht weiter mit Führungsfragen zu beschäftigen: «*Diese Organisation und auch die Betriebsökonomie interessiert den durchschnittlichen Richter einfach nicht*». Die juristische Arbeit steht bei Richtern klar im Vordergrund, während das Management und die Führung eher als etwas Sekundäres oder gar Niedriges beurteilt werden (siehe Emery/de Santis, Kapitel 2). Oftmals wird in diesem Zusammenhang von einem Spannungsverhältnis oder gar einer Unvereinbarkeit zwischen Qualitätsanforderungen an die Rechtsprechung und der mit Management-Ansätzen verbundenen Forderung nach Effizienz gesprochen.

Allgemein lässt sich daraus schliessen, dass das Bewusstsein eines Mehrwerts von Management sowie von Führung im Speziellen bei den Richtern häufig nicht vorhanden ist. Im Gegenteil wird die Führung, gerade weil sie oft mit zwingenden Direktiven und Hierarchie gleichgesetzt wird, mit nachteiligen Auswirkungen für die Qualität richterlicher Arbeit assoziiert. Direkte Führung wird oftmals als illegitimer und unerwünschter Einfluss in die Rechtsprechung und damit als Verletzung der richterlichen Unabhängigkeit gedeutet. Nur selten werden dabei auch positive Aspekte der Führung genannt. Bei der Einführung und Anwendung neuer Managementansätze sei immer viel Überzeugungsarbeit notwendig: «*Die Öffnung gegenüber dem Management wird langsam ablaufen, es gibt eine richtige Allergie demgegenüber*».[163] Die Erfahrung eines Gerichtspräsidenten bei der Einführung einer organisationalen Änderung ist: «*Am Anfang gibt es immer Widerstand. Aber nach einem halben Jahr war es dann akzeptiert*». Allgemein brauche es «*viel Erfahrung und zweitens grosse* 208

[161] «*Le travail d'un juge est de rendre des jugements et non d'organiser le fonctionnement*».

[162] «*Le juge de base ne s'intéresse pas au fonctionnement administratif de son tribunal*».

[163] «*L'ouverture au management va évoluer lentement, il y a une vraie allergie à ça*».

Überredungskunst, um die Richter zum Konsens zu bringen bei einer organisatorischen Regelung».

5. Analyse und Diskussion der Ergebnisse

5.1 Charakteristiken der beruflichen Kultur der Richter

209 In einer professionellen Bürokratie wie der Justiz, wo die Funktionsweise der gesamten Organisation massgeblich von der beruflichen Kultur der Hauptakteure abhängig ist,[164] scheint es umso wichtiger, dass mögliche Führungsansätze eng in Bezug auf ihren organisationalen und kulturellen Kontext betrachtet werden.[165] Wenn man die relevanten Aussagen der Justizakteure analysiert, bestätigt sich die Vermutung einer dominanten beruflichen Kultur der Richter. Im ersten Teil der Analyse werden auf der Basis der Aussagen der Justizakteure Eigenheiten dieser Berufskultur identifiziert und im Zusammenhang mit der Frage der direkten Führung wiedergegeben. Widerstand zu neuen Führungsansätzen kann insbesondere dort erwartet werden, wo diese nicht mit der beruflichen Kultur und Werte der Richter vereinbar sind. Eine mögliche Führung von Richtern wird konfrontiert mit:

- **Kontroll- und Machtbedürfnis:** Richter werden in den Aussagen der Justizakteure oft als *«Machtmenschen»* oder *«Häuptlinge»* charakterisiert, d.h. als Personen mit grossem Macht- und Kontrollbedürfnis. Sie wehren sich oftmals gegen die Zentralisierung von Entscheidungskompetenzen, da sie gerne immer und überall mitreden und damit ihren Einfluss sichern wollen. Ebenfalls bekunden Richter gemäss den Aussagen Mühe darin, Aufgaben zu delegieren. Man kommt zum Schluss, dass eine Entscheidung nur in Form eines Konsenses im Rahmen einer basisdemokratischen Entscheidungsfindung, wo jede Richterperson die gleiche Stimme hat, auf sichere Akzeptanz stosst. Eine Zentralisierung von Entscheidungskompetenzen und damit eine Hierarchisierung unter Richtern scheint kaum akzeptiert. Dies gilt auch für den Falle des Gerichtspräsidenten als „Primus inter pares". Eine gewisse Hierarchie unter Richterkollegen kann sich, wie bei Kiener[166]

---

[164] Vigour (2008).
[165] Orazi et al. (2013).
[166] Kiener (2001), S. 339.

angesprochen, höchstens aufgrund persönlicher Merkmale wie Autorität, Berufserfahrung oder Alter einer Richterperson ergeben, nicht aber aufgrund formeller Führungspositionen. Damit bestätigt sich die Annahme von Mosimann,[167] dass Richter in Führungspositionen trotz ihrer Führungsverantwortung nicht als formelle Vorgesetze der anderen Richter gelten, da sie vom gleichen Wahlorgan in die gleiche Funktion gewählt worden sind. Statt einer formellen Art der direkten Führung muss man wenn dann eher von einer kollegialen Führung sprechen.

– **Überbetonung der richterlichen Unabhängigkeit:** Ausser Frage steht, dass die personenbezogene Unabhängigkeit des Richters als wichtige Schranke jeglichen unerlaubten Einflusses auf die richterliche Tätigkeit gelten muss.[168] Obwohl viele Experten der Meinung sind, dass die richterliche Unabhängigkeit im administrativen Bereich der reinen Unterstützung der Justizverwaltung nicht gelten kann,[169] findet diese Unterscheidung in der untersuchten Praxis kaum statt. Mit einer Überbetonung ihrer Unabhängigkeit wehren sich Richter oftmals gegen jegliche Art der Einflussnahme. Das kann so gedeutet werden, dass die richterliche Unabhängigkeit von Richtern teilweise *strategisch* als Mittel dazu benutzt wird, um sich jeglicher Führung zu entziehen. Gemäss Crozier und Friedberg[170] hängt die Macht eines Akteurs in einer Organisation davon ab, wie dieser seine Ressourcen in den jeweiligen Interaktionen einsetzen kann, um seinen Freiheits- und Verhandlungsspielraum gegenüber anderen Akteuren zu erhalten oder zu erweitern.[171] Das Verhalten des Akteurs wird dabei als Strategie beschrieben, mit dessen Hilfe er Freiräume und Schwächen im Organisationssystem zu seinen Gunsten gezielt ausnutzen kann. Die in der Praxis sonst schon schwierige Unterscheidung zwischen dem richterlichen und dem administrativen Führungsbereich, welche zentral ist für die Frage der Legitimität richterlicher Führung, wird zusätzlich dadurch erschwert, dass Richter ihre Ressource der richterlichen Unabhängigkeit gezielt als Mittel zur Vergrösserung ihres Handlungsspielraumes

167 MOSIMANN (2013), S. 12.

168 VALOIS (2012).

169 CAVELTI (2013).

170 CROZIER/FRIEDBERG (1979).

171 *«Die Macht ist also letztlich in dem Freiraum angesiedelt, über den jeder der in eine Machtbeziehung eingetretene Gegenspieler verfügt, das heisst, in seiner mehr oder weniger grossen Möglichkeit, das zu verweigern, was der andere von ihm verlangt»* (CROZIER & FRIEDBERG, 1979, S. 41).

einsetzen und Führung generell als Eingriff in ihre Unabhängigkeit werten, bzw. werten lassen.

- **Individualistische Arbeitsweise:** Richter, in den Aussagen der Justizakteure unter anderem als *«eigenbrötlerisch»*, *«extrem individualistisch»*[172] oder *«freie Elektronen»*[173] beschrieben, zeichnen sich durch sehr individualistische und heterogene Arbeitsweisen aus. Deshalb sehen sich besonders solche Instrumente, welche auf die Harmonisierung der Arbeitsmethoden zielen, mit grossem Widerstand konfrontiert. Die direktive Führung im Bereich der richterlichen Arbeitsweise wird relativ einseitig nur von nicht-richterlichen Justizakteuren als wünschenswert erachtet. Dies entspricht der typischen Eigenschaft einer professionellen Bürokratie.[174] Experten üben ihre Funktion sehr unabhängig aus und benutzen ihre Kompetenzen nicht identisch wie ihre Kollegen. Man kommt zum Schluss, dass es allgemein sehr schwierig ist, Richter gewissen Harmonisierungen bezüglich ihrer Arbeitsweise zu unterwerfen. Mit solchen Eingriffen wird ihr Freiraum[175] reduziert, wogegen sie sich wie bereits erwähnt mit einer Überbetonung ihrer Unabhängigkeit wehren. Dieser Individualismus führt laut einiger Befragten zu Defiziten bei der Zusammenarbeit und Kommunikation.
- **Einseitiger Fokus auf richterliche Kompetenzen:** Ein fast vollständiger Konsens herrscht bei den befragten Justizakteuren darüber, dass Führungskräfte ihre Legitimität bei den Richtern nicht nur aufgrund ihrer Fachkenntnisse innerhalb der Justiz oder gar ihrer Führungskompetenzen erhalten, sondern hauptsächlich aufgrund dem rechtlichen Ausbildung und richterlichen Berufserfahrung. Die Aussagen deuten darauf hin, dass eine Führungskraft bei fehlender Zugehörigkeit zur richterlichen Berufskategorie keine reelle Chance auf Akzeptanz bei den anderen Richtern finden kann. Dies bestätigt wiederum das Bild einer dominanten Berufskategorie, welche die Kontrolle der Justiz als homogene Einheit unter sich ausmachen möchte. Ein zu starrer und einseitiger Fokus auf technische Kenntnissen und Fähigkeiten, welcher typisch ist für eine professionelle Bürokratie, kann eine Vernachlässi-

172 *«Extrêmement individualistes».*
173 *«Électrons libres».*
174 MINTZBERG (1982).
175 CROZIER/FRIEDBERG (1979).

gung von anderen wichtigen Kompetenzen wie derjenigen der Führungskompetenzen und Teamarbeit zur Folge haben.[176]

– **Desinteresse und Misstrauen gegenüber Management:** Die Abgrenzung der Richterschaft gegenüber allem Nicht-Richterlichen zeigt sich auch in einem Desinteresse oder einer teilweisen Ablehnung gegenüber Fragen zur Funktionsweise des Gerichts oder Führungsfragen im Speziellen. Die Erfüllung der richterlichen Tätigkeit gilt als Kernaufgabe, weshalb andere Aspekte daneben als eher unwichtig oder störend empfunden werden. Auch scheint das Verständnis zu herrschen, dass Führungskompetenzen nicht erlernt werden müssen, sondern bereits von der Praxis vermittelt werden. In den Aussagen der Richter konnte zudem ein allgemeines Misstrauen gegenüber Managementansätzen und insbesondere gegenüber Begriffen der Führung als hierarchische Einflussnahme festgestellt werden. Dies könnte auf das von der Studie von Cameron et al.[177] identifizierte Misstrauen der Richter gegenüber „Non-professionals“, aufgrund unterschiedlicher beruflicher Werte und Kultur von Managern und Richtern/Juristen, zurückgeführt werden. Eine so stark ausgeprägte Berufskultur wie bei den Richtern kann gemäss Vigour[178] ein bedeutendes Hindernis für neue Entwicklungen darstellen, da neue Regeln als Bedrohung gewertet werden. Die vorliegende empirische Untersuchung zeigt, dass gerade bei der Einführung neuer Ideen und Konzepte bei der Richterschaft oftmals ein *«enormer Widerstand»*[179] herrscht. Daher müsse laut Aussage immer zuerst die Angst und Abwehrhaltung vor Reform-Bestrebungen überwunden werden (*«Angst der Veränderung besiegen».*[180])

5.2 Diskussion der Hypothesen zur Führung von Richtern

Im Folgenden werden aufgrund der identifizierten Eigenheiten 210
der beruflichen Kultur der Richter überspitzte und teilweise provokante Hypothesen formuliert. Weiter sollen diese auf Basis der Analyse der Aussagen diskutiert und wenn möglich relativiert werden, um schlussendlich ein Fazit zu den Chancen und Herausforderungen einer direkten Per-

---

176 Festa/Walmsley (2005).

177 Cameron et al. (1987).

178 Vigour (2008).

179 *«Résistance énorme».*

180 *«Vaincre la peur de changement».*

sonalführung von Richtern zu ermöglichen. Die Hypothesen werden wiederum nach den Elementen der Definition einer direkten Personalführung strukturiert (Wer? Was? Wie? Wozu?).

A) Wer kann Richter führen?

Hypothese 1: <Richter haben keinen Vorgesetzten, weshalb sie nicht geführt werden können>

211 Auf Basis der in der Literatur genannten Erwägungen sowie den Erkenntnissen unserer Analyse lässt sich festhalten, dass sich der Richter im Verhältnis zum Gerichts- oder Abteilungspräsidenten nicht in einer wie in sonstigen Unternehmen üblichen Unterordnungsbeziehung befindet.[181] Doch ist deshalb eine direkte Führung ausgeschlossen? Nur weil es sich hier nicht um ein alltägliches Vorgesetzen-Mitarbeiter-Verhältnis handelt, heisst dies nicht, dass es gar keine direkte Führung geben kann. Die Frage ist vielmehr, welche Art der Führung möglich ist. Gemäss dem kontextabhängigen Führungsansatz ist eine Führung dann erfolgreich, wenn sie sich an die spezifische Situation anpasst und die Legitimität, die Akzeptanz und das Vertrauen der Gefolgschaft besitzt.[182] Im Kontext der Richter muss eine Führung also vereinbar sein mit der richterlichen Unabhängigkeit und gleichzeitig von den Richterkollegen akzeptiert werden. Es stellt sich besonders die Frage nach dem idealen Verhältnis zwischen Informalität und hierarchischer Struktur[183], also einer rein informellen und kollegialen Führung durch einen Richterkollegen oder einer mehr hierarchischen Weisungskompetenz eines Vorgesetzten.

212 Eine formelle Art der Personalführung stellt die Dienstaufsicht dar, welche in den meisten Gerichten im Rahmen rechtlich geregelter Verfahrensabläufe durch ein unabhängiges, richterliches Aufsichtsorgan ausgeübt wird. Die Dienstaufsicht kann jedoch nur die disziplinarischen Aspekte einer Führung abdecken, d.h. extreme Ausnahmefälle von offensichtlich fehlerhafter Amtsausübung.[184] Die Zwangsmittel der Dienstaufsicht entfalten zudem ein hohes Druckpotential auf die Richter und damit auf ihre Unabhängigkeit, weshalb hier das Anwendungsgebiet stark einge-

[181] CAVELTI (2013).

[182] AUSTRALIAN PUBLIC SERVICE COMMISSION (2013).

[183] MOSIMANN (2013), S. 14.

[184] KIENER (2001), S. 301.

schränkt ist.[185] Die formelle Dienstaufsicht kann eine direkte Personalführung, welche die Aktivierung der Motivation und Leistungsbereitschaft sowie das Engagements der Mitarbeiter zum Ziel hat, nicht ersetzen. Sie kann nur in Ausnahmefällen von krass fehlerhaften Verhaltensweisen zur Sicherstellung der Verfahrensfairness mit formell-rechtlich geregelten Zwangsmitteln eingreifen.

Obwohl man auch durch eine informelle und kollegiale Führung eine gewisse Führungsverantwortung ausüben kann, könnte ein Minimum an Struktur und formeller Führung die Beteiligten entlasten und der richterlichen Führungsperson mehr Klarheit über ihre Kompetenzen als „Primus inter pares" verschaffen. Diese Klarheit scheint heute oftmals zu fehlen.[186] Die Wahrnehmung von mehr formeller Führung liege auch im Interesse der Richterschaft, da gemäss Kettiger[187] sonst klare Regeln und Verantwortungen fehlen. Das zu drohende *Führungsvakuum* soll aufgrund des notwendigen Handlungsspielraums des Gerichts nicht von Aufsichts- und Oberaufsichtsorganen wahrgenommen werden, sondern liege in der Verantwortung der direkten Führung des Gerichts. Für eine Entwicklung hin zu einer formelleren Führung ist unbedingt auch die Akzeptanz der Richterschaft notwendig. Diese ist aber gemäss dieser empirischen Untersuchung nicht als allzu gross einzuschätzen. 213

Hypothese 2: <Richter in Führungspositionen müssen sich keine zusätzlichen Führungskompetenzen aneignen. Richterliche Praxiserfahrung und juristisches Wissen genügen für die Ausübung ihrer Funktion>

Die empirische Untersuchung bestätigt die Annahme, dass Führungspersonen im Gericht ihre Legitimation als Führungskraft nur aufgrund ihrer fachlichen, d.h. juristischen und richterlichen Fähigkeiten und Erfahrung, und kaum aufgrund von Führungskompetenzen erhalten. Die Aussagen der Justizakteure zeigen zudem, dass viele Richter generell nicht an Weiterbildungen im Bereich Management und Führung interessiert sind. Andere sind der Meinung, dass sie solche Kompetenzen nicht unbedingt benötigen oder diese bereits durch Praxiserfahrung abgedeckt werden. 214

---

185 Gemäss WITTRECK (2013) dürfen daher Erledigungszahlen nicht mithilfe der Disziplinarmassnahme gerügt werden. Der dadurch ausgeübte Erledigungsdruck zu einer zeitsparenden Arbeitserledigung kann dazu führen, dass nicht allen entscheidungsrelevanten Fragen nachgegangen wird und somit die Rechtsprechung in ihrer Unabhängigkeit gefährdet ist.

186 MOSIMANN (2013), S. 15.

187 KETTIGER (2003), S. 188.

Management- und Führungskompetenzen werden oftmals als unwichtig und im Vergleich zum Juristischen als etwas Niedriges gewertet.

215 An diese Stelle muss aber betont werden, dass viele Justizakteure in den Interviews durchaus die Wichtigkeit solcher Managementkompetenzen betont haben. Gerade Richter in Führungspositionen sowie administrativ Verantwortliche beschäftigen sich im Gegensatz zu den restlichen Richterpersonen aufgrund alltäglicher Herausforderungen durchaus mit Fragen zur Führung. Jedoch scheint es oftmals an den entsprechenden Kompetenzen zu fehlen. Die Personalentwicklung als wichtige Führungsaufgabe fand in den Gesprächen mit den Justizakteuren eine grosse Aufmerksamkeit. Hier kann auf die Wichtigkeit der Funktion eines „hybrid manager" gemäss der Studie von Byrkjeflot and Jespersen[188] verwiesen werden. Richter in Führungspositionen können zwischen beiden Welten des richterlichen Berufsstands und des Managements vermitteln und übersetzen, was gerade bei den grossen Unterschieden in Kultur und Werten zentral ist.[189] Dafür braucht es sowohl Einblicke und Kenntnisse des richterlichen Berufs sowie eben auch im Bereich des Managements und der Führung. Und auch eine minimale Bereitschaft der betroffenen Akteure, sog. *Konventionen* mit übergeordneten Zielen zu erstellen.

216 Aus den Aussagen der Richter lässt sich schliessen, dass diese nur dann zu einer Weiterbildung bereit sind, wenn Führungskurse auf die spezifischen Bedürfnisse der Richter zugeschnitten sind. Mit dem Zertifikatslehrgang „Judikative" der Richterakademie hat man auch bereits die Wichtigkeit eines solchen Lehrgangs erkannt und umgesetzt. Es spricht vieles dafür, dass das Bewusstsein für die Wichtigkeit von Weiterbildung vorhanden ist. Die Frage ist vielmehr, ob man Richter dazu zwingen kann, solche Weiterbildungen zu absolvieren oder ob es in der Selbstbeurteilung jedes Richters selbst liegt, seine individuellen Entwicklungsbedürfnisse zu erkennen.

B) Was soll geführt werden, d.h. in welchem Aufgabenbereich soll die direkte Personalführung von Richtern stattfinden?

Hypothese 3: <Die richterliche Unabhängigkeit schützt den Richter in jedem Bereich seiner Arbeit vor Eingriffen und Einflussnahme durch die direkte Personalführung>

188 BYRKJEFLOT/JESPERSEN (2014).
189 BOLTANSKI/THÉVENOT (1991).

Direktive Führung und die Zentralisierung von Entscheidungskompetenzen zu Gunsten der Richter in Führungspositionen darf nur dort ein Thema sein, wo die mögliche Gefährdung der richterlichen Unabhängigkeit ausgeschlossen werden kann. Nicht legitim ist die Führung im Bereich der Rechtsprechung, also in der Begründung und Motivation des einzelnen Urteils.[190] Die vorliegende empirische Untersuchung bestätigt, dass kein klarer Konsens über die Grenzen der Tragweite der richterlichen Unabhängigkeit im Bereich der organisatorischen und administrativen Tätigkeit existiert. Richter scheinen zudem dazu zu neigen, den Bereich, welcher von der richterlichen Unabhängigkeit erfasst wird, grösser zu deuten. Damit verweigern sie sich einem möglichen Einfluss in ihren Handlungsspielraum. 217

Die personenbezogene richterliche Unabhängigkeit darf jedoch nicht als Freiheitsrecht des Richters interpretiert werden, sondern als grundrechtlicher Anspruch jeder Prozesspartei auf Zugang zu einem unabhängigen Gericht.[191] Die richterliche Unabhängigkeit rechtfertigt demnach nicht jedes beliebige Verhalten des Richters. Dies gilt umso mehr im administrativen und organisatorischen Bereich, welcher die Unterstützung einer effizienten und effektiven Selbstverwaltung der Justiz betrifft. Der Richter ist dazu verpflichtet, seinen Beitrag zur Erfüllung des Leistungsprinzips der Justiz beizutragen.[192] In dem Sinne wird in der Literatur im Bereich rein administrativer Führungsprozesse im Gegensatz zum Bereich der Rechtsprechung eine gewisse Abkehrung vom „Primus inter pares“ Konzept verlangt,[193] hin zu einer mehr hierarchischen Struktur, wo Führung auch mit Weisungen erlaubt sein muss. 218

Ein besonders grosser Widerstand der Richter wurde gemäss vorliegender Untersuchung bei zwingenden Vorgaben auf operativer Ebene, d.h. im Bereich der richterlichen Arbeitsweise und bei individuellen Leistungsbeurteilungen, festgestellt. Von einer fehlenden Akzeptanz bei den Richtern sind somit insbesondere transaktionale, managementorientierte Führungsaufgaben betroffen. Ein umso grösseres Bedürfnis nach Führung besteht im Bereich der personenbezogenen Führungsaufgaben wie der Kommunikation, des Feedbacks und der Personalentwicklung. Diese ge- 219

---

190 TANQUEREL (2014).
191 POLTIER (2011), S. 1018 ff.
192 MOSIMANN (2013).
193 WIPFLI (2006).

hören in der öffentlichen Verwaltung gemäss Schedler und Proeller[194] zu besonders wichtigen und oftmals vernachlässigten Führungsinstrumenten.

C) Wie können Richter geführt werden?

Hypothese 4: <Eine richterliche Führung ist gleichzusetzen mit Selbstführung und Selbstorganisation>

220 Auch wenn sich ein Richter in Führungsposition durch juristische, richterliche sowie Kompetenzen im Bereich der Führung auszeichnet, bleibt die Überbetonung von Unabhängigkeit und Individualismus in der richterlichen Arbeitsweise eine grosse Herausforderung. Unter den Richtern herrscht ein starker Widerstand gegenüber jeglichem Zwang und zwar, so scheint es, unabhängig vom jeweiligen Tätigkeitsbereich. So argumentieren einige Richter, dass eine mögliche Führung unter keinen Umständen durch zwingende Instrumente und Weisungen erfolgen kann. Jeder Richter sei selbst dafür verantwortlich, seine Defizite in Arbeitsorganisation, Kompetenzentwicklung, Leistungserbringung und Motivation zu erkennen und allenfalls geeignete Massnahmen anzuordnen. Dieses Konzept entspricht der Idee des bereits eingeführten Richterportfolios, welches auf der reinen Selbstevaluation der Richter basiert, die komplett unabhängig von der Personalführung ist.[195]

221 Es ist jedoch zu bezweifeln, dass durch eine Selbstevaluation bei jedem Richter die vorhandenen Defizite genüg erkannt und die nötigen Entwicklungsmassnahmen ausgelöst werden. Auch wenn man davon ausgeht, dass die Selbstführung der Richter im Zentrum steht, braucht es dennoch jemanden, welcher die Richter mit Ideen einer effizienten Selbstführung konfrontiert, sie für die organisationalen Ziele sensibilisiert und zu Massnahmen im Bereich Personalentwicklung ermutigt. Die Personal- und Potenzialentwicklung stellen zentrale Aufgabe der direkten Personalführung dar.[196] Mosimann[197] plädiert dafür, dass im kollegialen, gerichtsinternen Austausch die individuellen Stärken und Schwächen kein Tabu sein dürfen und dass jedem Richter seine Pflicht im Rahmen des Leistungsauftrages des Gerichts durch einen fairen, individuellen Beitrag an der Bewältigung der Geschäftslast bewusst sein muss. Richter sollen ermuntert werden, nicht nur ihre fachlichen, sondern auch ihre sozialen

---

194 Schedler/Proeller (2009).

195 Lichti Aschwanden (2010).

196 Thom/Ritz (2000).

197 Mosimann (2013), S. 15.

Kompetenzen zu pflegen und weiter zu entwickeln. Schedler und Proeller[198] sehen die Rolle des modernen Leaders als Coach, welcher nicht primär Sachaufgaben kontrolliert, sondern die Mitarbeiter zu Leistung und Entwicklung motiviert.

222 Es ist davon auszugehen, dass transaktionale Führungs- und Kontrollinstrumente auf operativem Niveau wie Zielvereinbarungen, Leistungskontrollen oder Leistungsanreize aufgrund der fehlenden Akzeptanz eher schwer durchsetzbar sind. Führung ist jedoch nicht gleichzusetzen mit Kontrolle und zwingenden Direktiven. Auch die Kommunikation von Visionen, Zielen und Werten gehören gemäss den transformationalen und instrumentellen Führungsansätzen zu wichtigen Führungsaufgaben, welche die organisationale sowie individuelle Leistung der Mitarbeiter positiv beeinflussen. Wie bereits Kellis und Ran[199] in ihrer Studie argumentierten, scheint gerade die Möglichkeiten eines moderneren Ansatzes von Führung, welcher sich auf gemeinsame Werte und Ziele statt auf organisationale Autorität und Kontrolle fokussiert, geeigneter zu sein für das komplexe Umfeld der Justiz. Weiter könnte die partizipatorische Führung aufgrund des basisdemokratischen Führungsverständnisses im Richterkollegium einen hohen Stellenwert besitzen. Richter müssen aufgrund ihres Expertenwissens, ihrem Wille zur Mitwirkung an Entscheidungen und der schwachen formellen Legitimität der Führungskraft in möglichst viele Entscheidungen miteinbezogen werden. Ein kooperativer und partizipativer Führungsstil scheint dem Kontext in den meisten Fällen wohl am besten angepasst.[200] Hier wäre eine tiefergehende Analyse notwendig, um genauer definieren zu können, welche Entscheidungen konkret einen demokratischen Prozess voraussetzen und wo allenfalls auch eine mehr direktive Entscheidungsfindung möglich ist.

D) Wozu sollen Richter geführt werden?

Hypothese 5: <Eine Reform im Bereich der direkten Führung von Richtern führt nur zu zusätzlichem bürokratischem Aufwand und hat negative Einflüsse auf die Qualität der Rechtsprechung>

223 Tatsächlich scheint bei den Richtern im Allgemeinen ein grosses Misstrauen gegenüber Managementmethoden und insbesondere jeder Art von Führungskultur zu herrschen. Der Mehrwert von Führung geht gegenüber

[198] SCHEDLER/PROELLER (2009), S. 235.
[199] KELLIS/RAN (2012).
[200] DUBS (2005).

der Betonung negativer Assoziationen grösstenteils unter. Zu nennen sind Befürchtungen vor mehr Hierarchie, Machtverlust, Widersprüche zur Qualität der Rechtsprechung oder unnötigem bürokratischen Aufwand, welche die Richter von ihrer Kernaufgabe ablenken. Selbst wenn man sich darüber einig wäre, dass eine Veränderung im Bereich der direkten Führung für eine effiziente Selbstverwaltung der Justiz notwendig ist, lässt das allgemeine richterliche Misstrauen und der Widerstand solche Reformen als unmöglich erscheinen.

224 Das Ziel einer effektiven Führung ist es nicht, die richterliche Unabhängigkeit einzuschränken, sondern diese zu stärken.[201] Eine direkte und teilweise formellere Führung von Richtern kann laut Kettiger [202] zur Sicherstellung einer effizienten Justizverwaltung und damit auch der Qualität richterlicher Arbeit beitragen. Den Richtern muss klar vermittelt werden, dass gewichtige Funktionsfehler in der Gerichtsführung einen negativen Einfluss auf die Qualität der Justiz, konkret auf die Rechtsprechung und die richterliche Unabhängigkeit, haben können.[203] Doch wie ist eine solche Reform möglich, wenn sie von der Mehrheit der Richter nicht als sinnvoll oder legitim erachtet wird? Denn neben geeigneten Führungsinstrumenten braucht es auch die Bereitschaft und Akzeptanz der Richter, administrative Anordnungen nicht gleich als Eingriff in die richterliche Unabhängigkeit zu qualifizieren.

225 Die dominante berufliche Kultur der Richter ist ein äusserst wichtiger Faktor, welcher in die Strategie einer möglichen Entwicklung im Bereich der Führung miteinbezogen werden muss. Ein solcher Kulturwandel würde die Gesamtheit der Werte, Einstellungen und Verhaltensweisen der Richter betreffen. Er kann nur erfolgreich sein, wenn Führungskräfte auf Basis der bisherigen kulturellen Elemente neue Werte und handlungsleitende Konzepte entwickeln, die den zukünftigen Aufgaben der Justiz Rechnung tragen.[204] Es sollen nicht einfach privatwirtschaftliche Entwicklungen übernommen, sondern diese an die bestehende Kultur angepasst werden. Hier anzusprechen ist die Studie von Byrkjeflot and Jespersen,[205] welche in der Praxis eine Verschmelzung und Anpassung von Management-Logiken mit der traditionellen Kultur des Berufsstandes beobachtet.

---

201 LIENHARD/ KETTIGER/WINKLER (2012), S. 2.
202 KETTIGER (2003).
203 TANQUEREL (2014).
204 THOM/RITZ (2000), S. 96.
205 BYRKJEFLOT/JESPERSEN (2014).

Dadurch entstehen spezifische Formen hybrider Kulturen, wobei sich die Akteure an die sich teilweise widersprechenden Werten, Prinzipien und Regeln mithilfe kreativer Strategien anzupassen versuchen.[206] Kulturwandel führt einerseits zu einem Lernprozess der beteiligten Individuen durch eine gezielte Veränderung der Motivations- und Qualifikationskomponenten und andererseits trägt der Kulturwandel zu einer erhöhten Innovationsfähigkeit auf allen Ebenen des Reformprozesses bei.[207]

Gerade die transformationale und instrumentelle Führung spielen gemäss Leadership-Forschung eine wichtige Rolle bei der Durchführung eines organisationalen Wandels.[208] Dazu gehört, dass eine realistische Vision und Ziele kommuniziert werden, welche bei den Mitarbeitern auf Verständnis, Identifikation und Vertrauen stossen. Mit dem transformationalen Leadership kann ein Leader Veränderungen der Wertevorstellungen, Bedürfnisse und Fähigkeiten seiner Follower bewirken.[209] Die Vision soll schlussendlich in konkrete strategische und taktische Pläne umformuliert und die Mitarbeiter bei ihrer persönlichen Zielerreichung unterstützt und gefördert werden. Das instrumentelle Leadership will die Leistung der Mitarbeiter dadurch fördern, dass die Zielerreichung durch Monitoring und Feedback begleitet und gefördert und nicht wie beim transaktionalen Leadership korrigierend oder belohnend eingegriffen wird.[210] Dies entspricht eher dem Kontext der Richter, wo zwar ein Bedürfnis nach mehr Feedback vorhanden ist, aber ein grosses Misstrauen gegenüber individuellen Leistungskontrollen und -Beurteilungen herrscht. Im Allgemeinen soll die Führung den Richtern das „Wozu“ (den Mehrwert) einer direkten Führung näher bringen. Indem Führungsansätze den Richtern klar und verständlich kommuniziert werden, können laut Dubs[211] Ängste, welche von einem veralteten, zu hierarchischen Führungskonzept herrühren, verringert werden. In eine ähnliche Richtung argumentiert Fairholm,[212] welcher betont, dass ein tieferes Verständnis von verschiedenen Leadership-Ansätzen wichtig ist, um die Akzeptanz und Legitimation von Führung in öffentlichen Organisationen wie der Justiz zu erhöhen. 226

---

206 EMERY/GIAUQUE (2014).
207 THOM/RITZ (2000)S. 92.
208 ANTONAKIS (2006).
209 BASS (1994).
210 ANTONAKIS (2006), S. 13.
211 DUBS (2005).
212 FAIRHOLM (2004), S. 587.

6. Fazit und Ausblick

6.1 Berufliche Kultur der Richter als Herausforderung für die direkte Personalführung

227 Die Diskussion über die Möglichkeit und die konkrete Ausgestaltung einer direkten Führung von Richtern ist weitgehend durch Uneinigkeit geprägt. Einerseits herrscht ein grosses Misstrauen seitens der Richter gegenüber jeglicher Führungskultur, da diese oftmals als unvereinbar mit der richterlichen Unabhängigkeit interpretiert wird. Anderseits gibt es in der Literatur wie auch in der Praxis zahlreiche Stimmen, welche für eine stärkere Wahrnehmung der formellen Führung im administrativen und organisatorischen Tätigkeitsbereich der Richter plädieren.[213] Die empirische Analyse hat ergeben, dass die Ausübung der Führungsverantwortung eines Richters gegenüber seinen Richterkollegen nicht nur durch rechtliche Prinzipien, sondern zusätzlich durch die dominante richterliche Berufskultur eingeschränkt wird. Gemäss der empirischen Untersuchung zeichnet sich die Persönlichkeit der Richter durch ein grosses Autonomie- und Machtbedürfnis, einer individualisierten Arbeitsweise, Widerstand gegenüber jeglicher Art von Beeinflussung, einer starken Orientierung auf rein juristische Aspekte und einem generellen Desinteresse und Misstrauen gegenüber „Non-Professionals" aus. Dies setzt klare Grenzen für die Definition einer möglichen direkten Personalführung. Sie lassen einem sogar daran zweifeln, ob eine Solche überhaupt möglich sei. Dies wäre jedoch ein vorschneller und zu eindimensionaler Schluss auf die Forschungsfrage und würde der Realität in Schweizer Gerichten nicht gerecht werden. Wie die Analyse gezeigt hat, gibt es durchaus Richter, welche sich für Führung interessieren, ihre Notwendigkeit anerkennen und die Führungsverantwortung auch wahrnehmen. Die entscheidende Frage ist, wie genau eine solche Führung angesichts der kulturellen und rechtlichen Grenzen im Kontext der Richter aussehen kann. Bei der Ausübung von Führungsverantwortung ist man stets mit der Frage konfrontiert, ob man sich im Bereich der Unterstützung der Selbstverwaltung der Justiz befindet oder ob man Einfluss auf die richterliche Arbeit im Sinne der Rechtsprechung nimmt. Im zweiten Fall wird eine Personalführung aufgrund der Unvereinbarkeit mit der richterlichen Unabhängigkeit verhindert. Diese wichtige Abgrenzung des juristischen vom administrativen Bereich

[213] KETTIGER (2003), CAVELTI (2013).

scheint sowohl in der Theorie wie auch in der Praxis alles andere als klar definiert zu sein. Es handelt sich hier nicht nur für das Thema der direkten Personalführung sondern für das Justizmanagement im Allgemeinen um eine äusserst zentrale Frage, welche nach weiteren Recherchen und Konkretisierungen verlangt.[214]

6.2 Entwicklungspotenziale im Bereich Leadership

Die Analyse zeigt, dass die Führung von Richtern kaum auf hierarchische Weise im Sinne zwingender Weisungsbefugnisse und zentralisierter Entscheidungskompetenzen von Führungsverantwortlichen umgesetzt werden kann. Dafür fehlt bei den Richtern die nötige Akzeptanz. Die Ausübung eines transaktionalen Leaderships mit Einführung von formal-organisatorischen Führungsinstrumenten wie Zielvereinbarungen, Leistungskontrollen und zwingenden Arbeitsstandards scheinen nur möglich, wenn sich dazu ein Konsens unter den Richtern finden lässt. Dieser Aufsatz vertritt die Meinung, dass die Aufgaben von führenden Richtern eher bei Aufgaben der transformationalen und instrumentellen Führung liegen. Hier lassen sich mehr Freiheiten und Entwicklungsmöglichkeiten für eine direkte Führung von Richtern finden. Eine Führung ist dann effektiv, wenn die Mitarbeiter ihr vertrauen, sich mit ihren Visionen und Zielen identifizieren können und intrinsisch motiviert sind, sich im Sinne der organisationalen Ziele zu engagieren.[215] Solche organisationalen Ziele der Justiz werden im Rahmen von Justizreformen zur Bewältigung der gestiegenen Arbeitslast und Anforderungen formuliert. Diese beinhalten konkret die Steigerung der Qualität und Effizienz, eine strengere Ressourcenverwaltung, das Anbieten kundenfreundlicher Dienstleistungen sowie eine erhöhte Rechenschaftspflicht und Transparenz unter gleichzeitiger Stärkung der richterlichen Unabhängigkeit und der damit verbundenen Qualität der Rechtsprechung.[216] 228

Zudem hat die empirische Untersuchung ergeben, dass ein grosses Bedürfnis nach mehr Kommunikation unter den Richtern aber auch mit anderen Justizmitarbeitern besteht. Weiter existiert der Wunsch nach einer stärker ausgeprägten Feedbackkultur und nach Förderung der richterlichen Teamarbeit. Dabei sind in erster Linie persönlich-interaktionelle Füh- 229

214 PRIGIONI (2014).
215 ANTONAKIS (2006), S. 11.
216 LIENHARD et al. (2012), ENCJ (2012).

rungsinstrumente wie das regelmässige Mitarbeitergespräch zur Personalförderung und –Entwicklung sowie ein kritisches (Leistungs-)Feedback zur Unterstützung der individuellen Arbeitsleistung von grosser Bedeutung. Dazu gehört auch die Kommunikation der Aspekte einer effizienten und qualitativ hochstehenden Selbstverwaltung der Justiz sowie dem Mehrwert der direkten Personalführung im Gericht. Die Richter sollen ihren Beitrag zu einer „guten" Justiz erkennen und leisten, wofür sie auch gewisse nicht-juristische, administrative Verantwortungen wahrnehmen müssen. Die direkte Personalführung befindet sich dabei in der Rolle des Coachs, welcher die Richter zur effizienteren und effektiveren Selbstorganisation ermutigt und anleitet.

230 Eine Führung scheint nur dann angemessen, wenn sie sich an einem möglichst partizipativ und kooperativ ausgestalteten Führungsstil orientiert. Eine Chance könnte in der Umsetzung des vor allem im Kontext der Schule erwähnten „distributed, shared leadership" liegen. Dahinter steckt die Idee, dass eine komplexe Organisation wie z.B. die Schule nicht durch nur einen Schulleiter geleitet werden kann. Vielmehr sollen Lehrer ebenfalls Führungsaufgaben übernehmen und die Führungskraft bei Führungsentscheidungen unterstützen.[217] Im Kontext des Gerichts würde dies bedeuten, dass die führende Richterperson die anderen Richter dazu motiviert, selbst Führungsverantwortung im Umgang mit ihren Mitarbeitern zu übernehmen und die dazu notwendigen Kompetenzen anzueignen. Dieses „Empowerment" der Richter mit eigenen Führungsaufgaben kann wiederum helfen, ihre Leistung und Job-Zufriedenheit zu verbessern. Zudem eignen sie sich dabei gemäss der Studie von York-Barr und Duke[218] ein besseres Verständnis der Funktionsweise der Organisation an und entwickeln eine positivere Sichtweise und mehr Offenheit gegenüber neuen Herausforderungen und der Entwicklung neuer Führungsmethoden. Zur Bestätigung dieser Erkenntnisse sind allerdings zusätzliche Recherchen notwendig.

---

[217] Van Ameijde/Nelson/Billsberry/van Meurs (2009), S. 766, Grandjean Lüthi (2010).

[218] York-Barr/Duke (2004), S. 282.

6.3 Unterschiedliche Strategien für einen erfolgreichen Kulturwandel

Aufgrund des grossen Misstrauens von richterlicher Seite gegenüber Managementreformen sollte man gut analysieren, wie ein Kulturwandel im Hinblick auf ein stärkeres Bewusstsein für die Notwendigkeit von Führung erreicht werden kann. Im Bereich der Organisationsentwicklung kann zwischen zwei verschiedenen Strategien unterschieden werden[219]. Gemäss dem evolutionären Ansatz der Organisationsentwicklung müssen sich zuerst die Einstellungen, Werte und Verhaltensweisen der Mitarbeiter ändern, bevor sich das System selbst wandeln kann, also bevor konkrete Führungskonzepte und –Instrumente implementiert werden können.[220] Bevor eine Akzeptanz für konkrete Instrumente und Konzepte erreicht wird, muss in der Organisation zuerst ein allgemeines Veränderungspotenzial geschaffen werden. Dafür spricht die Aussage eines Richters: *«Man muss bei einem Teil der Juristen intervenieren und versuchen, ihre Mentalität zu ändern».*[221] Die andere Strategie besagt, dass die Systementwicklungen zuerst gesetzlich verankert und formalisiert sein müssen, bevor eine Akzeptanz dafür entstehen kann.[222] In den Gesprächen wird oftmals erwähnt, dass Richter am konkreten Beispiel sehen müssen, dass etwas funktioniert und dass ein Instrument keine Bedrohung für ihre Autonomie darstellt, bevor sie es akzeptieren. Auch die hohe rechtliche Durchstrukturierung und das Bedürfnis nach Transparenz und Rechtssicherheit würden eher für den zweiten Strategieansatz sprechen. Es könnte daher von Vorteil sein, vor der definitiven Einführung von Führungsinstrumenten im Rahmen von Pilotversuchen deren Akzeptanz zu fördern oder Führungskompetenzen und Aufgaben zuerst in einem Geschäftsreglement festzuschreiben. Lienhard ist auch der Meinung, dass mögliche Kompetenzen der Gerichtspräsidien zur Durchführung richterlicher Leistungsbeurteilungen durch justizorganisationsrechtlichen Grundlagen geregelt sein müssen. [223] Nur so verfügen diese über die notwendige demokratische Legitimation und Führungsverpflichtung. Ebenfalls in diese Richtung zielt die Aussage eines Gerichtspräsidenten, welcher erklärt, dass mit 231

---

219 STAINES (1996).

220 THOM/RITZ (2000), S. 108.

221 *«Il faut intervenir sur (une partie) de la population de juristes et essayer de changer les mentalités».*

222 STAINES (1996), S. 38 ff.

223 LIENHARD (2014).

dem schriftlichen Festschreiben der Kompetenzen die Akzeptanz für seine Rolle als Präsident gestiegen sei.[224] Welche Strategie besser ist, kann dieses Kapitel nicht beantworten, da es Argumente für beide Seiten gibt. Staines[225] kommt in seiner Fallstudie zur Entwicklung von Managementreformen in Spitäler zum Schluss, dass die Formalisierung von konkreten Instrumenten und Prozessen nur dann erfolgreich ist, wenn sie durch einen Wandel der Organisationskultur unterstützt wird. Eine wichtige Rolle spielt dabei wiederum die Direktion des Gerichts, also Richter in Führungspositionen, welche den Richterkollegen den Mehrwert einer direkten Führung anhand von Beispielen aus dem richterlichen Alltag klar und verständlich kommunizieren.[226]

6.4 Grenzen der Methodik und Forschungsausblick

232 Die für den Artikel ausgewählten und analysierten Aussagen repräsentieren zwar einen breiten Querschnitt aller Argumente, entsprechen jedoch nicht einer vollständigen Analyse aller gesammelten Daten. Zudem kann mit der hier angewendeten induktiven Methodik (siehe Punkt 3) die Verteilung und Gewichtung der Argumente nicht evaluiert und die Ergebnisse nur eingeschränkt generalisiert werden. Da nur zwei Deutschschweizer Kantone, das Tessin sowie alle Welschschweizer Kantone untersucht wurden, gelten die hier gemachten Aussagen nicht als repräsentativ für alle Schweizer Gerichte und für alle Richter. Auch können die gezogenen Schlüsse nicht für die gesamte Schweizer Justiz verallgemeinert werden. Das Ziel dieser Arbeit war es, Aussagen und Hypothesen zur Führung von Richtern herauszufiltern. Diese könnten in einer weiteren Forschung mithilfe einer repräsentativen Methodik getestet werden. Ein interessantes Vorhaben für die Zukunft wäre es, die in diesem Artikel formulierten Ideen und Hypothesen Richtern und Gerichtspräsidenten von Schweizer Gerichten zu präsentieren und ihre Reaktion und Meinungen einzufangen. Je nach spezifischem Kontext sind verschiedene Modelle für die Führung von Richtern vorstellbar. Dabei sollte den jeweiligen Kompe-

---

[224] *«Es gab schon vor mir einen Kantonsgerichtpräsidenten, er war der Kammerpräsident und der war schlussendlich der Chef, aber das stand nirgends so richtig. Und dann war auch niemand wirklich zuständig für die Kanzlei, was nur solange gut ging, wie sie keine Probleme hatten und gut miteinander auskamen.»*.

[225] STAINES (1996), S. 77.

[226] STAINES (1996), S. 33.

tenzen und persönlichen Eigenschaften der Richter in Führungspositionen und den zu führenden Richtern Rechnung getragen werden.

7. Literaturverzeichnis

Antonakis, J. (2006). Leadership: What is it and how it is implicated in strategic change? *International Journal of Management Cases, 8*(4), 4-20.

Australian Public Service Commission (2013). *Thinking about leadership: a brief history of leadership thought.*

Bass, B. M. (1994). Improving organizational effectiveness through transformational leadership. Thousand Oaks: Sage Publications.

Bass, B. M. (1998). Transformational Leadership: Industrial, Military, and Educational Impact. Mahwah. NJ: Lawrence Erlbaum Associates.

Bird, C. (1940). *Social Psychology*. New York: Appleton Century.

Boltanski, L. and L. Thévenot (1991). De la justification. Les économies de la grandeur. Paris, Gallimard.

Bouckaert, G. (2007). Cultural Characteristics From Public Management Reforms Worldwide. In K. Schedler & I. Proeller (Hrsg.), *Cultural Aspects of Public Management Reform* (Bd.16, S. 29-64). UK: Elviers.

Broussine, M. (2003). Public Leadership. In T. Bovaird & E. Löffler (Hrsg.), *Public Management and Governance*. London, New York: Routledge.

Byrkjeflot, H., & Jespersen, P. K. (2014). Three conceptualizations of hybrid management in hospitals. *International Journal of Public Sector Management, 27*(5).

Cameron, J. D., Zimmermann, I. M., & Downling, M. S. (1987). *The Chief Justice and the Court Administrator: The Evolving Relationship.* Williamsburg: National Center for State Courts.

Campell, J. P., Marvin, D. D., Lawler, E. E., & Weick, K. E. (1979). *Managerial Behavior, Performance and Effectiveness*. New York: McGraw-Hill.

Cavelti, U. (2013). Der Gerichtspräsident - primus inter pares oder Justizmanager? In P. Mäusli-Allenspach & M. Beusch (Hrsg.), *Steuern und Recht - Steuerrecht!* (S. 325-332). Basel: Helbing Lichtenhahn Verlag.

Crozier, M., & Friedberg, E. (1979). *Macht und Organisation. Die Zwänge kollektiven Handelns*. Königsstein: Athenäum Verlag.

Denhardt, J.-V., & Denhardt, R. B. (2003). *The New Public Service: Serving, Not Steering*. Armonk, NY: M.E.Sharpe.

Drucker, P. F. (1998). *The Leader of the Future*. San Francisco: Jossey-Bass.

Dubs, R. (2005). *Die Führung einer Schule. Leadership und Management.* Zürich: Verlag SKV.

Emery, Y. & Giauque, D. (2014). Introduction: L'univers hybride de l'administration au XXIe siècle. *Revue internationale des Sciences Administratives*, 80(1), 25-34.

Emery, Y. and L. deSantis (2014). "What Kind of Justice Today? Expectations Of 'Good Justice', Convergences And Divergences Between Managerial And Judicial Actors And How They Fit Within Management-Oriented Values." International Journal for Court Administration 6(1): 63-75

Emery, Y. (2015). Quels freins culturels au management de la justice en Suisse? In Sammlung Justizforschung, Band 2

Emery, Y. (2012). "La diversité des motivations des employés publics. Recherche exploratoire dans un contexte post-bureaucratique en Suisse." Revue française d'administration publique 142(2): 491-515

European Network of Councils for the Judiciary (ENCJ), (2012). *Judicial Reform in Europe*. Report 2011-2012, 1-28.

Fairholm, M. (2004). Different Perspectives on the Practice of Leadership. *Public Administration Review, 64*(5), 577-590.

Fernandez, C. F. (2005). Developing and Testing an Integrative Framework of Public Sector Leadership: Evidence from the Public Education Arena. *Journal of Public Administration Research and Theory, 15*(2), 197-217.

Festa, M. S., & Walmsley, J. (2005). Clinical Leadership in Hospital Care. *BMJ: British Medical Journal, 331*(7509), 161-162.

Giauque, D. and Y. Emery (2008). Repenser la gestion publique. Lausanne, Presses polytechniques et universitaires romandes.

Grandjean Lüthi, F. (2010). *Le leadership des directions d'établissment scolaire: Vers une optimisation par des pratiques de Gestion des Ressources Humaines*. L'Harmattan.

Grütter, M. (2012). Leitungskompetenzen in der Justiz. *"Justice - Justiz - Giustizia" Richterzeitung, 2012/3.*

Hill, H. (2006). Von Good Governance zu Public Leadership. *Verwaltung und Management, 12*(2), 81-84.

Hollmann, J. (2010). *Führungskompetenz für Leitende Ärzte. Motivation, Teamführung, Konfliktmanagement im Krankenhaus.* Berlin, Heidelberg: Springer-Verlag.

Holmes, M., & Shand, D. (1995). Management Reform: Some Practitioner Perspectives on the Past Ten Year. *Governance, 8*(4), 551-578.

Jenkins, W. (1947). A Review of Leadership Studies with Particular Reference to Military Problems. *Psychological Bulletin, 44*(1), 54-79.

Kellis, D. S., & Ran, B. (2012). Modern leadership principles for public administration: time to move forward. *Journal of Public Affairs, 13*(1), 130-141.

Kettiger, D. (2003). *WOV in der Justiz – ein Balanceakt zwischen Effizienz und Rechtsstaatlichkeit* (Bd. 44). Bern: Verlag SGVW.

Kiener, R. (2001). *Richterliche Unabhängigkeit. Verfassungsrechtliche Anforderungen an Richter und Gerichte.* Bern: Stämpfli Verlag

Kirkpatrick, I., S. Ackroyd, et al. (2005). The New Managerialism and Public Service Professions. Basingstoke, Palgrave McMillan.

Klages, H. (1998). Erfolgreich führen und motivieren! In D. Wagner (Hrsg.), *Personal und Personalmanagement in der modernen Verwaltung* (S. 51-67). Berlin: Duncker & Humblot.

Klopfer, R. (2007). Vom Richter zum Justizmanager. In M. Heer & A. Urwyler (Eds.), *Justiz und Öffentlichkeit* (S. 13-21). Bern: Stämpfli.

Kolb, M. (2008). *Personalmanagement. Grundlagen - Konzepte - Praxis.* Wiesbaden: Gabler.

Lichti Aschwanden, N. (2010). Das Weiterbildungssystem "Richterportfolio" im Kanton Zürich: Konzept und erste Erfahrungen. *"Justice - Justiz - Giustizia" Richterzeitung, 2010/2.*

Lienhard, A., (2005). *Staats- und verwaltungsrechtliche Grundlagen für das New Public Management in der Schweiz: Analyse – Anforderungen – Impulse*. Bern: Stämpfli-Verlag.

Lienhard, A., (2007). Controllingverfahren des Bundesgerichts. *"Justice - Justiz - Giustizia" Richterzeitung, 2007/2.*

Lienhard, A., (2009). Oberaufsicht und Justizmanagement. *"Justice - Justiz - Giustizia" Richterzeitung, 2009/1.*

Lienhard, A., (2014). Leistungsbeurteilung in der Justiz, in: *Thomas Stadelmann/Stephan Gass/Richard McCombe* (Hrsg.), Richterliche Unabhängigkeit und Leistungsbeurteilung, Die Beurteilung richterlicher Tätigkeit im Spannungsverhältnis zur richterlichen Unabhängigkeit im europäischen Vergleich, Zürich/St. Gallen, S. 15-44.

Lienhard, A., & Kettiger, D. (2011). Keine Absage an ein zeitgemässes Justizmanagement. *"Justice - Justiz - Giustizia" Richterzeitung, 2011/2.*

Lienhard, A., Kettiger, D., & Winkler, D. (2012). Status of Court Management in Switzerland. *International Journal For Court Administration*, IJCA 2012 Special Issue, 1-27.

Ludewig, R. (2008). Der Umgang mit dem richterlichen Ich-Ideal: Der Mensch hinter dem Richter. In M. Heer (Hrsg.), *Der Richter und sein Bild. Wie sehen wir uns - wie werden wir gesehen?* (S. 25-44). Bern: Stämpfli-Verlag.

Mahon, P., & Schaller, R. (2013). Le système de réélection des juges: évidence démocratique ou épée de Damoclès? *"Justice - Justiz - Giustizia" Richterzeitung, 2013/1.*

Mansour, F. (2013). Olivier Jornot suspecté de «putsch judiciaire», *Le Temps*, 22.11.2013.

Martens, P. (2013). Le management modifie-t-il le rapport du juge à sa profession? In Larcier (Hrsg.), *Quel Management pour quelle justice?* (S. 107-122): Thierry Marchandise.

Martineau, S. (2005). L'observation en situation: enjeux, possibilités et limites. *Recherches qualitatives, Hors Série* (2), 5-17.

Mintzberg, H. (1982). *Structure et dynamique des organisations*. Paris: Les Editions d'Organisation.

Mosimann, H.-J. (2011). Leistungsbeurteilung von Richterinnen und Richtern - Qualitätsmerkmal oder Angriff auf die richterliche Unabhängigkeit? *"Justice - Justiz - Giustizia" Richterzeitung, 2011/1.*

Mosimann, H.-J. (2013). Richterliche Unabhängigkeit und Leistungsbeurteilung. *Beurteilung richterlicher Tätigkeit im Spannungsverhältnis zur richterlichen Unabhängigkeit*, St. Gallen: Schweizerische Vereinigung der Richterinnen und Richter, SVR.

OECD. (2001). *Public Sector Leadership for the 21st Century.* Paris

Park, S. M., & Rainey, H. G. (2008). Leadership and Public Service Motivation in U.S. Federal Agencies. *International Public Management Journal, 11*(1), 109-142.

Poltier, E. (2011). L'organisation et le fonctionnement interne de l'ordre judiciaire et des tribunaux. *AJP/PJA, 8*, 1018-1036.

Poltier, E. (2012). Le pouvoir judiciaire "s'administre lui-même". *"Justice - Justiz - Giustizia" Richterzeitung, 2012/3.*

Prigioni, M.-C. (2014). *Le management de juridiction: Analyse comparative de l'organisation et du fonctionnement managérial de cinq juridictions du pouvoir judiciaire genevois.* Masterarbeit, MPA IDHEAP, Université de Lausanne, Lausanne.

Raselli, N. (2011). Richterliche Unabhängigkeit. *"Justice - Justiz - Giustizia" Richterzeitung, 2011/3.*

Schedler, K., & Proeller, I. (2009). *New Public Management* (Bd. 4). Bern, Stuttgart, Wien: Haupt Verlag.

Spillane, J. P. (2012). Distributed leadership. New Jersey, John Wiley & Sons

Sohm, S. (2007). *Zeitgemässe Führung - Ansätze und Modelle. Eine Studie der klassischen und neueren Management-Literatur*: Bertelsmann Stiftung.

Staines, A. (1996). *L'approche "Gestion totale de la Qualité" dans les hôpitaux publics. Situation actuelle et perspectives d'avenir.* Masterarbeit, MPA IDHEAP, Université de Lausanne, Lausanne.

Stogdill, R. (1974). *Handbook of Leadership: A survey of Theory and Research.* New York: Free Press.

Strauss, A., & Corbin, J. (2004). *Les fondements de la recherche qualitative: techniques et procédures de développement de la théorie enracinée*. Fribourg: Academic Press Fribourg.

Tanquerel, T. (2014). *Avis de droit relatif aux compétences de la Commission de haute surveillance du Tribunal cantonal vaudois et en particulier à la portée à donner à l'exception de l'indépendance juridictionnelle contenue à l'article 135 de la Constitution vaudoise*.

Thom, N., & Ritz, A. (2000). *Public Management. Innovative Konzepte zur Führung im öffentlichen Sektor*. Wiesbaden: Gabler.

Tschümperlin, P. (2009). Die Aufsicht des Bundesgerichts. *Schweizerische Juristen Zeitung*, (10), 233-243.

Van Ameijde, J. D. J., Nelson, P. D., Billsberry, J., & Van Meurs, N. (2009). Improving leadership in Higher Education institutions: a distributed perspective. *Higher Education, 58*(6), 763-779.

Van Wart, M. (2003). Public-Sector Leadership: An Assessment *Public Administration Review, 63*(2), 214-228.

Valois, M. (2012). *L'indépendance judiciaire. La justice entre droit et gouvernement*. Zürich: Schulthess Verlag.

Vigoda-Gadot, E., & Golembieski, R. T. (2001). Citizenship behaviour and the spirit of new manageralism: a theoretical framework and challenge for governance. *American Review of Public Administration, 32*(3), 273-295.

Vigour, C. (2008). Ethos et légitimité professionnels à l'épreuve d'une approche managériale: le cas de la justice belge. *Sociologie du travail, 50*, 71-90.

Vroom, V. H., & Jago, A. G. (1988). *The New Leadership: Managing Participation in Organizations*. Prentice Hall: Englewood Cliffs, NJ.

Wice, P. B. (1995). Court Reform and Judicial Leadership: A Theoretical Discussion. *The Justice System journal, 17*(3), 309 - 321.

Wipfli, H. (2006). *Justizmanagement am Beispiel eines Steuergerichts. Struktur, Organisation und Führung*. Master, Universität Bern, Bern.

Wittreck, F. (2013). Erledigungszahlen unter (Dienst-)Aufsicht? *Deutsche Richter Zeitung DRiZ, 2*, 60-61.

York-Barr, J., & Duke, K. (2004). What Do We Know About Teacher Leadership? Findings From Two Decades of Scholarship. *Review of Educational Research, 74*(3), 255-316.